2006

Hooked Rugs Today

Amy Oxford
Photography by Cynthia McAdoo

Holidays
Geometrics
People
Animals
Landscapes
Accessories
and More

Schiffer Publishing Ltd ®

4880 Lower Valley Road Atglen, Pennsylvania 19310

The photographs of Cosette Allen and of her rug "The Parsonage at Star Island" are courtesy of Ted Allen.

Rug measurements have been rounded off to the nearest inch while miniature rugs have been rounded to the nearest quarter inch.

The Green Mountain Rug Hooking Guild's rug show is not juried. Any of our members can be a part of the exhibit. Similarly, this book embraces all of our guild members, including experienced rug hookers, beginners, and children.

Every possible attempt to properly identify and acknowledge the names of rug designers and pattern companies has been made by both the rug hookers and the author. If needed, corrections can be made to future editions as long as the author is notified.

Front cover images (clockwise, from bottom left): In the Kingdom of Justice: Memorial For All Who Perished in New Orleans. Designed and hooked by Burma Cassidy; *Megan's Valentine.* Designed and hooked by Kathi Hopper; *Penny Prayer Rug.* Designed and hooked by Maddy Fraioli; *Chicken Soup.* Hooked by Janet C. Berner, designed by Yankee Peddler; *Spring Pocketbook.* Designed and hooked by Lesa Morrissey; *East Ironbound Squares.* Design adapted and rug hooked by Judith Dallegret.

Back cover images (clockwise, from left): Art. Designed and hooked by Donna Beaudoin; *Cats' Paws, Lambs' Tongues and Dog Eared.* Designed and hooked by Suzi Prather; *Three Nights at Duncan's.* Hooked by Jennifer Manuell, designed by Deanne Fitzpatrick; *Bird Stocking.* Designed and hooked by Lesa Morrissey; *Sheep Shoulder Bag.* Hooked by Gail Majauckas, designed by Underhill Farm.

Copyright © 2007 by Amy Oxford
Library of Congress Control Number: 2006936831

Designed by "Sue"
Type set in Cataneo Lt BT/Arrus BT

ISBN: 978-0-7643-2636-3
Printed in China

Other Schiffer Books by Amy Oxford
Hooked Rugs Today
Punch Needle Rug Hooking: Techniques and Designs

Other Schiffer Books on Related Subjects
Hooked on Rugs: Outstanding Contemporary Designs, by Jessie A. Turbayne
The Big Book of Hooked Rugs: 1950-1980s, by Jessie A. Turbayne
The Complete Guide to Collecting Hooked Rugs: Unrolling the Secrets, by Jessie A. Turbayne
The Hooker's Art: Evolving Designs in Hooked Rugs, by Jessie A. Turbayne
Hooked Rug Treasury, by Jessie A. Turbayne
Hooked Rugs: History and the Continuing Tradition, by Jessie A. Turbayne
Contemporary Hooked Rugs: Themes and Memories, by Linda Rae Coughlin

Can you find this cricket? It is hiding in one of the rugs. Hint: It's on the bottom.

Published by Schiffer Publishing Ltd.
4880 Lower Valley Road
Atglen, PA 19310
Phone: (610) 593-1777; Fax: (610) 593-2002
E-mail: Info@schifferbooks.com

For the largest selection of fine reference books on this and related subjects, please visit our web site at **www. schifferbooks.com**
We are always looking for people to write books on new and related subjects. If you have an idea for a book please contact us at the above address.

This book may be purchased from the publisher.
Include $3.95 for shipping.
Please try your bookstore first.
You may write for a free catalog.

In Europe, Schiffer books are distributed by
Bushwood Books
6 Marksbury Ave.
Kew Gardens
Surrey TW9 4JF England
Phone: 44 (0) 20 8392-8585; Fax: 44 (0) 20 8392-9876
E-mail: info@bushwoodbooks.co.uk
Website: www.bushwoodbooks.co.uk
Free postage in the U.K., Europe; air mail at cost.

Contents

The companion volume to this book features Green Mountain Rug Hooking Guild Honoree Pat Merikallio; the 2005 and 2006 Viewers' Choice Award winners; and rugs from the following categories: "strong women," Orientals, florals, Twelve Days of Christmas, children's rugs, architectural designs, abstracts, miniature Russian punch needle embroidery, and additional animals (cats, birds, sheep, cows, and wild animals).

"Be careful not to work too hard—remember how happy koalas are, and they only break from napping in order to eat!"
—Lucy Soutter (Amy's sister)

Dedication

This book is dedicated to the memory of our friend, Cosette D. Allen, 1942-2005.

Cosette's greatest enthusiasm was creating hooked rugs. Over the twenty years that she hooked rugs, she became an artist and created many beautiful rugs that she distributed among her family, also donating rugs to several causes to be auctioned off for charity. She was most proud of her rug, "The Parsonage at Star Island," which was chosen as one of the fifteen best original design rugs of 2004 by *Rug Hooking* magazine and published in their annual *Celebrations* edition. Our guild is proud to have known her. She is greatly missed.

The Parsonage at Star Island. Designed and hooked by Cosette D. Allen. 35" by 27".
Cosette planned this rug for at least five years. The parsonage was her favorite building on Star Island, a Unitarian-Universalist Conference Center at The Isles of Shoals off Portsmouth, New Hampshire. The walls of the building are hooked from the same piece of brown and gray plaid wool that she saved for at least three years for that specific purpose while she assembled the rest of the wool and planned the rug. She worked from a photograph that she took of the building during a conference on the island. Her goal was to make the rug entirely from recycled wool, but she finally broke down and dyed a 6" by 8" piece of new wool to get just the right shade of pink for the flowers.

Acknowledgments

I would like to gratefully acknowledge everyone who made rugs for this book. If, as the saying says, "even the longest journey begins with a single step," then surely the longest rug begins with a single loop. I am very grateful that you made that first loop and kept going.

Thank you to friend and photographer, Cynthia McAdoo, who has the ability to turn the worst kind of tedium into something to laugh about, and I mean laugh until you have tears streaming down your face. When we had to double-check that all 910 rugs in this two book set were in their right places, it required double checking two sets of numbers for each rug—1,820 numbers in all. Cynthia would read me the numbers while I checked them on the computer. I gradually started falling into a coma. To keep me awake she started singing me the numbers in an assortment of ridiculous falsetto and bizarre voices, to the tune of "Camptown Races" and other popular favorites. The additional things she did to keep up morale are too silly and numerous to list.

Sincere thanks to my editors, Tina Skinner and Donna Baker, for their expertise and guidance; to rug show co-chairs Rae Harrell and Barbara Held for making the show so beautiful; to Shelburne Museum and Museum President Stephan Jost for making us feel so welcome; to Museum's Visitor Services Manager Bruce Andrews, for making the show run so smoothly; and to Monty Stokes for all his work behind the scenes.

Many thanks to the marvelous guild volunteers who braved the cold to help with the photo shoot: Nancy Baker, Angelika Brumbaugh, Carolyn Buttolph, Janet Conner, Cheryl Connor, Jerry Connor, Judith Dallegret, Eugenie Delaney, Judith English, Liam English, Fiona Fenwick, Pandy Goodbody, Jane Griswold, Jocelyn Guindon, Joan Hebert, Priscilla Heininger, Layne Herschel, Stephanie Krauss, Gail Lapierre, Rachelle LeBlanc, Kevin McLoughlin, Ruth McLoughlin, Celia Oliver, Linda Pitkin, Karen Tompson, and Lin Watson.

All of the rug makers' information and quotes featured here were typed thanks to the generosity and skill of Nancy Bachand, Nancy Baker, Gail Lapierre, Bonnie LaPine, Jane Ploof and Maureen Yates. I am very thankful for their hard work. Special thanks to Maureen Yates for helping me to format all the information, and transfer it to my computer.

Sincere thanks to Green Mountain Rug Hooking Guild president Anne-Marie Littenberg for allowing me to include her article, "Rug Hooking, Past and Present." Anne-Marie also compiled the "Vendor List" and "Suggested Reading" list and carefully proofread the final manuscript. Her help was invaluable. With Anne-Marie as president, the guild is in good hands.

Love and thanks to my mother, Julie Righter, for proofreading the book with such an eagle eye, for giving me confidence, and for letting me know I could be whatever I wanted when I grew up, as long as I was happy. Who knew that I would become a rug hooker and that you would be correcting such a large home work assignment?

I am grateful to Judy English for making countless phone calls to rug hookers, and for cheerfully helping me make sure everyone was included in the index. Thanks also to Shirley Zandy and Maureen Yates for helping with the index; to Preston McAdoo for all the delicious meals and hospitality; to The Bailey Island Rug Hookers for giving me something to look forward to; to all of the rug designers and rug shop owners who assisted me; and to Ted Allen for generously providing the photographs for our dedication.

Thank you to Alaina Dickason, Jonathan Roberts, Iris Oxford, Andréa Borriello, Lynette Noble, Lindsay Boyer, Mark Boyer, Lucy Soutter, John Soutter, Mat Oxford, Madora Soutter, Brewster Righter, Lee and Gavin Greenewalt, Barb Moyer, Suzanne Sawyer, Oliver, Manuel, Courtney Clark, Don Riley, Ben Harper, The Heddwch Hookers, Geoff Gruender, and my trusty laptop, Harriet, who wasn't supposed to last this long.

Most of all, thank you to Peter Oxford.

This book is made possible by the many guild members who generously volunteered their time at the Hooked in the Mountains XI rug show. Wholehearted thanks to Jill Aiken, Polly Alexander, Sandy Alsum, Nancy Bachand, Nancy Baker, Donna Beaudoin, Jennie Behr, Nancy Birdsall, Kathy Boozan, Betty Bouchard, Angelika Brumbaugh, Diane Burgess, Sara Burghoff, Karen Bushey, Carolyn Buttolph, Shirley Chaiken, Willy Cochran, Janet Conner, Cheryl Connor, Sheila Coogan, Karen Cooper, Judith Dallegret, Eugenie Delaney, Suzanne Dirmaier, Judy Dodds, Lory Doolittle, Betty Edwards, Judith English, Fiona Fenwick, Maddy Fraioli, Diana Gauthier, Stephanie Gibson, Susan Gingras, Pandy Goodbody, Jane Griswold, Jocelyn Guindon, Rae Harrell, Joan Hebert, Priscilla Heininger, Barbara Held, Layne Herschel, Mary Hulette, Kathy Hutchins, Rachel Jacobs, Laurie Kass, Debra Kaiser, Diane Kelly, Stephanie Krauss, Cyndi LaBelle, Gail Lapierre, Bonnie LaPine, Jean LaPlant, Jen Lavoie, Rachelle LeBlanc, Diana Link, Sue Longchamps, Sherry Lowe, Anne-Marie Littenberg, Susan Mackey, Delbert Martin, Karen Martin, Raina Mason, Beth McDermett, Kris McDermett, Barbara McKenna, Ruth McLoughlin, Joan Mohrmann, Carol Munson, Fran Oken, Lynn Oconc, Celia Oliver, Bonnie Olson, Trinka Parker, Jane Perry, Carol Petillo, Nancy Phillips, Linda Pitkin, Jane Ploof, Bobbi Pond, Karen Quigley, Dot Rankin, Julie Rogers, Mary Sargent, Arlene Scanlon, Amy Spokes, Ruth St. George, Karen Tompson, Lin Watson, Johanna White, Helen Wolfel, Maureen Yates, Shirley Zandy, and the many other volunteers who jumped in to help at the last minute.

Introduction

Behind Barn Doors – A Look Inside The Rug Show

It was early on a raw, seventeen-degree Vermont spring morning, March 18, 2006, when hundreds of hooked rug makers arrived at the red Round Barn on the grounds of Vermont's Shelburne Museum, carrying armloads of rolled up rugs. People had driven from afar and flown in from all across the country. Many were delivering rugs for their entire rug hooking group, using the museum's garden cart to pull them up the small hill leading to the entrance. Long-distance friends happily greeted one another, and admired each other's handiwork. "I was up until two finishing this," said one tired woman. "Don't feel bad," someone else chimed in, "I hemmed mine in the car on the way here. What? No of course I wasn't driving!"

Shelburne Museum's Round Barn as seen through the eyes of rug hooker and photographer, Cynthia McAdoo. Thanks to Martha V. North whose rug "Dave and My Shadow" makes up the background. (Can you find Martha's shadow?) Thanks also to Davey DeGraff. Two of the trees from her rug "Maple View Farm" have been transplanted next to The Round Barn to provide some shade. Photograph of The Round Barn used in this collage © Shelburne Museum, Shelburne, Vermont.

You could see your breath inside the unheated barn. Volunteers in parkas, scarves, winter boots, hats, and gloves checked in the rugs, some of which had taken more than ten years to complete. The paperwork for each rug was checked, and a note was made not to use ballpoint pens next year. (Who knew the ink would freeze?) A few people forgot to include a photo of their piece but we were prepared, Polaroid camera in hand. Pictures were taken but they all remained the same shade of black. Apparently the film agreed with the ballpoints—it was just too cold.

Next, rugs from each of the different categories were taken to their own areas of the barn—the animal rugs were put here, Orientals there, florals in one corner, and landscapes in another, ready to be hung in their section of the show. There were mountains of rugs. Enough to keep many bugs snug for a long time. From the barn, guild members walked a short distance to the museum's Café for our biannual meeting. Guild news, an interesting guest speaker, and a delicious lunch were all enjoyed. The Polaroids even developed, as happy as we were to be warm.

At our Green Mountain Rug Hooking Guild's first exhibit, eleven years ago, we were afraid there might not be enough rugs. "Hook! Hook! Hook!" we were told by our worried president, hoping to avoid bare walls and a sparse display. On this freezing day in 2006, we didn't have this problem. An amazing 940 rugs were carried through the barn doors. "Stop! Stop! Stop!" we thought. "Where will we put them all?"

New walls were quickly built by volunteers to accommodate the hundreds of additional rugs we hadn't anticipated, and meanwhile, every rug was photographed for this two-volume book. Excellent natural lighting was required, so a plywood backdrop was assembled, just outside the barn door, in a little protected entryway out of the wind. The photo shoot took place from March 19-22. Everything went smoothly, except for a scare when the camera batteries died in the biting cold. Not wanting to panic the volunteers, the photographer kept the unsettling problem quietly to herself, tucked the batteries next to her skin under her five layers of clothing, and crossed her fingers. Luckily, the batteries thawed out and came back to life. They were carefully coddled for the rest of the shoot.

The photography had its own choreography involving still more volunteers. One person would wheel out the rugs in a red wagon, another hung a rug on the backdrop. An ID number was held up next to the rug, the camera clicked twice, someone else took the rug down, and yet another person put it back in the barn in its correct department. It was exciting to get a sneak preview of all the rugs, many of which brought our efficient crew to a complete standstill, everyone moving in closer for a better look. We took breaks in the museum's heated ladies' room, taking turns huddling around the hot air blower of the hand dryer. The camaraderie was cheerful, the lighting was perfect, we finished in four days, and luckily, the snow flakes didn't show up in the pictures.

Meanwhile, back in the barn, a crew of volunteers was hard at work. A large number of guild members would be arriving in a few days to hang the show, and the volunteers wanted to be ready for them. After much discussion, the largest rugs were hung on the silo that graced the center of the barn. Two men on tall ladders worked side by side, each holding one end of a heavy 4' by 6' floral. "Is this straight?" one of the men yelled down. "No, up a little on the left," came a reply from below. The overall effect was striking, but we knew some of the artists would be disappointed to have their work displayed at such heights. Where else could we put them?

On March 29-30, just eleven days after the rugs first arrived, dozens of volunteers returned to the historic barn for "the hanging." I heard one member ask, "Do we have to call it that? Who made up that terrible name anyway? It sounds like we're going to the gallows and should bring a noose!" Despite its somewhat dubious connotation, "the hanging" has become the name over the years that stuck for this two-day challenge of finding a spot for every rug. This year, there were two crews, one upstairs and one down, working with care and speed, coordinating styles, designs, colors, sizes, and patterns. Many workers wore snow pants and other ski-wear to stay warm. At midday, a wonderful homemade hot lunch was delivered by volunteers. The atmosphere was full of excitement, but also nervousness, as wall space dwindled. People worked in groups of two or three, laying out the rugs first for compatibility and spacing, then hanging them on the walls. A white antique canopy bed was brought in to hold all the pillows, and many "hangers" discovered a new

appreciation for the tiny space-saving miniature rugs, which all fit daintily on one wall. By the end of the effort, the barn was a breathtaking sight and every piece fit perfectly, like a 940 piece puzzle.

The opening reception was March 31. Volunteers arranged the dessert buffet, beverages, and flowers. A jazz duo played, the guild honorees were recognized, and visitors walked around in circles, literally, following the shape of The Round Barn that once held real cows, and now featured hooked ones. "Try walking around the circle in one direction and then go back the other way," one woman suggested, "You'll see the rugs you might have missed if you do."

For nine days, people streamed through the show. From April 1-9, the public visited, tour buses pulled in, and rug hookers came from near and far. School kids arrived in yellow buses, excited to be on a field trip, ready for a guided tour and lessons in "The Kids Hook Nook." The "Hooked in the Mountains" rug school held classes on the museum grounds, and students eagerly combed the vendor booths in the basement, searching for that perfect piece of wool for their class projects. Guild members demonstrated their craft on the middle floor, next to the popular giant heater that was installed for the show. Volunteers manned the front desk and worked at the guild table. Cameras flashed everywhere. "You know why there are so many rugs this year don't you?" one lady with a video camera explained to her friend, "It's because some woman's doing a book about the show and any guild member who puts a rug in the show can be in the book too. You can have five rugs in the show and they'll all be in the book. "Well, that explains it," said the friend, "Everyone wants to be in the book!"

It was four o'clock, April 9, the last day of the exhibit, and all the rug makers were anxious to grab their rugs and go home. "Are you going to the breakdown?" One guild member asked another. "Oh yes," she replied, "My husband and I always breakdown together." "Good grief, that sounds like you need a therapist! Who makes up these names?" a man laughed, hammer and screwdriver in hand, ready to start taking down the rugs. When the OK was given, several hundred guild members all carefully took down their own rugs, and the rugs of their friends. Meanwhile, the breakdown crew removed the carpet tack strips and other hardware that was used to hang much of the work. A show that took a year to plan, and days to hang, came down in a few short hours. A young woman wearing a paisley hand-hooked hat said, "Did you hear that the museum's gonna set up the heater earlier next year so we'll have it for the check-in and everything?" "Oh, that is good news!" said her friend as she packed up her tools.

A crew of volunteers signed out the rugs, and guild "bouncers" guarded the doors, checking receipts, making sure every rug went out safely in the right hands. A vanload of rugs was taken home by a volunteer, who promptly mailed them back to members living too far away to attend the show. In the end, all 940 rugs were carried back out through the big red front doors.

An audible sigh of relief was heard by the show co-chairs and all of the volunteers. Ninety-eight plywood walls and acres of track lighting were taken down and saved for next year. "The Kids Hook Nook" was emptied out, vendors packed up, The Round Barn was swept clean, and hundreds of rug makers drove home, already planning their next rugs, ready to do it all over again next year.

At the center of Shelburne Museum's Round Barn is a circular silo that was used for displaying a variety of hooked rugs at the Green Mountain Rug Hooking Guild's April, 2006 exhibition. Photograph © Shelburne Museum, Shelburne, Vermont.

Rug Hooking, Past and Present

"What do I have to do to exhibit my rug at the Green Mountain Rug Hooking Guild's annual show at Shelburne Museum?" is a question I am frequently asked. Also, "Is 'Hooked in the Mountains' a juried show? How do I know if my work is good enough to exhibit? I never learned the 'right' way to hook, so can my rug be exhibited? May I enter a rug if I used material other than pure wool strips, such as yarn?" One query came from an artist who focuses her work on creating rugs using shirring and yarn sewn techniques that were developed prior to 1840—before "traditional" rug hooking seems to have evolved.

Celebrating a broad range of experience (from self-taught to widely studied), and a diverse range of materials and techniques, is in the spirit of our earliest rug hooking ancestors, who hooked from their imaginations, utilizing whatever materials they had available. They did not buy patterns and kits. In fact, earliest hooked rugs were a craft of poverty.

At a time when textiles were some of the most valuable possessions a family could own (the early nineteenth century), ladies who pursued embroidery and quilting usually had a modicum of wealth to purchase threads, take embroidery lessons, etc. But hooked rugs were being created by people who had creativity, ingenuity, and not much else. Rugs created from about 1840 on were done on burlap backing because burlap was free—one used an old grain or feed bag, and a bent nail stuck into a wooden handle. Every and any scrap of fiber that was no longer usable as clothing or household linen was put into rugs.

It is interesting that in the United States, yarn was not a material of choice for hooked rugs, mostly because it was too precious and had to be saved for knitting and weaving. I recently saw a nineteenth-century Edward Sands Frost rug that was being restored. Much of the rug was originally hooked with cotton. Did this consist of leftover scraps from shirting or bedding? Grenfell mats were meticulously hooked with recycled jerseys, plus old silk and nylon stockings. William Winthrop Kent published a book in 1930 titled, *The Hooked Rug*. It details his understanding (some of it now disputed by contemporary scholars) about the history of hooked rugs. He described a yarn sewn rug with a backing of sailcloth that was done by a Captain Talpey during the War of 1812. In addition, Mr. Kent personally knew a sailor from Cape Cod who fashioned rugs from cotton strips pulled through sailcloth. Given this history, what conclusions can we draw about the "right" and "wrong" way to create rugs and mats? This book celebrates it all—from the perfectly pulled loops of cut wool used in commercial patterns, to the creative spirit of original designs done with new materials and techniques. A rug hooker may work using strictly prescribed techniques and materials. Or, one may pursue an original vision, pushing the creative envelope. Some create rugs to help decorate their homes; others, to commemorate important family events; and still others, to fulfill an artistic vision. All such pursuits are honored and celebrated by the Green Mountain Rug Hooking Guild.

—Anne-Marie Littenberg
President, Green Mountain Rug Hooking Guild

Chapter 1

2006 Green Mountain Rug Hooking Guild Honoree – Michele Micarelli

Every year the Green Mountain Rug Hooking Guild honors one or more of its members, recognizing their achievements and celebrating their creativity with a gala reception and a retrospective. Having these rugs at our annual hooked rug show is an inspiration to our members and visitors and gives us a chance to follow the progression and development of the featured artists' work. This year, three very talented rug hookers were chosen: Patricia Merikallio from Capitola, California; Michele Micarelli from New Haven, Connecticut; and Emily K. Robertson from Falmouth, Massachusetts. In addition to making award-winning rugs, all three woman are also well-loved rug hooking instructors, passing on to others the craft that is also their passion.

Since they are admired and respected equally, the only fair way to present our honorees is to list them alphabetically. Patricia Merikallio was featured previously in the companion volume to this book. Michele Micarelli is shown in Chapter 1 of this book, and Emily K. Robertson is highlighted in the next chapter, Chapter 2. We are proud to recognize all three of these outstanding guild members, and to applaud their artistry.

A Few Words From Michele

"What an honor it was to be chosen as one of the 'Strong Women!' However, I feel that I am just coming into my own style and that my best work is still in me. This is perhaps because I have committed myself to developing my imagination above all. I occasionally write stories, make Sailor's Valentines, and am currently making an altered book, among many other projects. I have a lust for learning, love to garden, tell jokes, decorate my home, and collect everything!"

"Rug hooking and teaching rug hooking have opened up a world of fun and travel to me. I have met the most amazing people. I have stayed at the homes of the most generous, funny, and talented people who quickly became friends. I have learned more from my students than I could have ever imagined; not just about fiber arts, but also life lessons. The places I have stayed have each been beautiful and unique. Among my favorites are: the shores of California and Maryland; Rugs By the Sea rug school with its beautiful Victorian houses called 'Painted Ladies' in Cape May, New Jersey; Peggy's Ranch in the Texas Hill Country; Edmonton, Alberta, and Burlington, Ontario in Canada. I am more than lucky."

"I am a certified rug hooking teacher whose main objective is to unleash creativity. The classes I teach are full of storytelling, imagination exercises, and laughter. I have been a rug hooker since 1991 and prefer using four and five cut wool, yarn, and linen for lots of detail."

"I started rug hooking because of childhood memories of rugs my father made while he was recovering from tuberculosis. In 1991, I was fortunate to find a generous teacher named Jeanne Zook who eventually encouraged me to join both A.T.H.A. (Association of Traditional Hooking Artists) and McGown guilds. She also encouraged me to teach. Since then, I have had many teachers at schools and workshops to whom I owe many thanks."

"My other loves are my fabulous and supportive husband, Anthony, two amazing children, and five high energy grandchildren. I am proud to have served on the A.T.H.A. Region 1 Board of Directors for more than ten years. I am currently President of the Northern McGown Teacher's Workshop. I am a judge at CraftAdventure in New England and I am thrilled to have had my rugs appear in several editions of the *Celebration of Hand-Hooked Rugs* series. I have also been a judge for *Celebrations* in the past."

"When I was a child, there were a few hooked rugs on the floor. I knew my father had made them during a long hospital stay for the treatment of tuberculosis. This intrigued me and when I was old enough I began searching for rug hooking supplies. I checked phone books when I traveled. I also spent eight years as a gift shop owner specializing in handcrafts, and five years as an antique dealer; all the while, I never even got a whiff of supplies anywhere. Yes, I saw the occasional old rug at a flea market, but the rug hooking world seemed to be a secret that was not revealing itself to me! Many years later, in 1991, while antiquing with my sister-in-law, Hart Caparulo, I came upon a beautiful farmhouse with a 'Rug Hooking Supplies' sign in front. Although it was the end of the day, I pleaded with Hart to stop. I was simply overcome with joy to find many rugs on display and more supplies than one could hope for in this beautiful shop, called Whispering Hill Farm. The real treat was that Donna Swanson, the owner, was willing to sit me down for a quick lesson. Then off I went with my bag of supplies and a list of hookers in my area that Donna had wisely dropped in my bag. Just a day later, I found a teacher in my area, Jeanne

Zook, who taught me to hook with swatches and spot-dyed wools. She helped me complete the pattern 'Ruthie' that I bought at Whispering Hill Farm from Donna."

"Soon after I hooked my first rug, I met Maggie McLea at a meeting and she recruited and trained me to be director of the A.T.H.A. Region 1 school in Madison, Connecticut. I instituted an annual auction as a fund raiser in which I was the auctioneer. Much to my shock, a pattern came up in the auction that was one of the patterns my father had hooked and that I had loved as a child. His rugs were long gone due to deteriorating burlap. Needless to say, I outbid everyone for this 'Scottie' pattern, source unknown, and hooked it with joy in only six weeks."

Honoree Michele Micarelli at the opening reception, March 31, 2006. The Round Barn, Shelburne Museum, Shelburne, Vermont.

"Much to my shock a pattern came up in the auction that was one of the patterns my father had hooked and that I had loved as a child. His rugs were long gone due to deteriorating burlap. Needless to say I outbid everyone for this 'Scottie' pattern..."

—*Michele Micarelli*

Rug show co-chair Rae Harrell painted signs for each of the show's three honorees to decorate and celebrate their portion of the show.

Scottie. Hooked by Michele Micarelli, New Haven, Connecticut. 26" by 36". Designer unknown.
"This same pattern was hooked by my father and was the source of my interest in rug hooking."

Ruthie. Hooked by Michele Micarelli, New Haven, Connecticut. 22" by 28". Designed by Pearl K. McGown.
"This was my first rug, made in 1991. Hooked with swatches, tasteful colors, and the help of my first teacher, Jeanne Zook."

Just Sittin'. Hooked by Michele Micarelli, New Haven, Connecticut. 28" by 20". Designed by Jane McGown Flynn.

"This is my 'McGown Chicken Challenge' rug. It was a fun challenge for a biennial rug show. Everyone got the same pattern but it could be altered and embellished in any way. The results were wonderful. Among the hundreds shown were bat-chickens, chickens with hats, kilts, grass skirts, G-strings, and chickens that were stuffed, feathered, prodded, and embroidered. The show chairman, Vicki Calu, built a chicken coop along with fiddle music and hay bales. It was great fun."

Below:
Ostintatia Monay. Designed and hooked by Michele Micarelli, New Haven, Connecticut. 24" by 20".

"This rug was designed in a most interesting class with Rae Harrell. Rae walked us through many steps of feeling the features of our faces and drawing them onto paper. When this exercise was complete, each person in class had a face with a touch of their own essence. The face I drew had the look of an exotic beautiful black woman. I hooked her in a way to suggest this, but in a stylized manner. When the face was complete, the next step was to look at the face and decide, 'where is she and what is her story?' I named her Ostintatia Monay, my inner black self! I decided she was a girl with a past, living in New Orleans and working in an elegant restaurant as the hostess. In the upper right, you can see a bit of the end of a neon sign that reads 'Cafe Anthony.' The leaded glass reflects the interior of the cafe where plants can be vaguely seen. The many layers of old New Orleans paint behind her are a great backdrop, as she has her picture taken by a tourist. She is unable to hide the sadness in her eyes, and her skull earrings give a hint of her Santeria and Voodoo upbringing."

Peacock Purse. Designed and hooked by Michele Micarelli, New Haven, Connecticut. 8" by 8". "Developed in a class with Kei Kobayashi."

Like all the exhibitors in the rug show, honorees are asked to describe their rugs in fifty words or less. When Michele Micarelli described her rug "Goddess" in only eleven, I wanted to know more. Michele had described the symbolism in this rug during the rug show opening reception, so I knew it was full of secrets. I asked her to talk about the real meaning of this piece:

"My rug 'Goddess' was meant to be a mandala. I loved the idea of a circle in a circle and continued to add even more circles. I drew and drew with quite a bit of abandon. At the time I had just read *The Da-Vinci Code,* and was intrigued by the idea of secrets and symbolism in artwork. I began to evaluate the kinds if things that might be symbols of me and my life. Some of them were quite intentional and some revealed themselves to me after they were drawn. Someone once told me my animal self was a dragon, so in went the magic dragon with wings holding up the circle. Humor is a great part of my life and also a most wonderful survival skill. The jester wrapped in palace pennant flags is my way of depicting this. The bug, scarab, is a symbol of abundance and survival, born from the surrounding fire. The sunrise is my devotion to the ecology, the clouds a hope for the preservation of the atmosphere. My husband and I belong to Greenpeace and I can often be heard chanting 'recycle, reuse, renew' to my grandchildren. The circle with my hand holding the sun is the creative side of me that is capable of everything. The babies wrapped in leaves are of course my children. Just to the right of them you can see the five birds, my grandchildren. The jewel shape over my head represents my intuition. The luna moth is a gift from my husband, who knew I would love such an amazing creature. The snake is temptation to excess, distraction, and not staying focused. Two red stars are my parents in opposite hemispheres, both influential, but never in tandem. Look, it's the whole universe, every star and planet representing so many friends. The paisleys are my teachers, the people who taught me life lessons, school lessons, and rug hooking. The peacock feathers are the side of me that loves to sing, dress up, tell a joke, and dance. The love of water and living near water is also present. Seashells have encrusted my ceilings as well as mesmerized me into making 'Sailor's Valentines.' In my ocean are four dolphins, my siblings, who saved me from drowning in an abusive childhood. No wonder I believe in magic! Most importantly, there is a dark, strong, steady, circle seemingly simple but so complex—look carefully at the colors. This is my husband keeping me contained with a big hug so I don't fly off into the ether!"

Goddess. Designed and hooked by Michele Micarelli, New Haven, Connecticut. 42" diameter. "The symbols of my world done in a mandala meditation circle."

Selvage. Designed and hooked by Michele Micarelli, New Haven, Connecticut. 24" by 30".
"Hooked entirely with selvages."

Juggler of Hearts. Hooked by Michele Micarelli, New Haven, Connecticut. 36" diameter. Designed by Michele Micarelli and Ralph Caparulo.
"My first original design, drawn with the help of my brother, Ralph Caparulo. Inspired by my juggling husband who carefully handles our hearts."

Creation. Designed and hooked by Michele Micarelli, New Haven, Connecticut. 9" by 9".
"Hooked in a workshop with Rae Harrell. A 'doodle' exercise."

Afternoon Delight. Hooked by Michele Micarelli, New Haven, Connecticut. 33" by 30". Designed by Michele Micarelli and Ralph Caparulo.
"This rug is my self-portrait. It was hooked when the challenge came from The Green Mountain Rug Hooking Guild to hook a rug with the theme 'You Are The Star.' It was great fun trying to capture myself in full color and grand size! My brother, Ralph Caparulo, is a fine artist and helped me draw this piece. I planned all the colors and dyed all the wool using dips, spots, swatches, and painted wool. I picked the purple for a royal touch and the yellow for the happy and whimsical feeling I was hoping to capture. Being opposites on the color wheel they really bounced. There are also bits of metallic fabrics, ribbons, and yarn added to the wool. The wonderful thing about hooking this rug was that it made me laugh every time I worked on it. That's almost ten months of laughing. The most difficult part was getting the already short, foreshortened thighs to look right!"

15

Solitude. Hooked by Michele Micarelli, New Haven, Connecticut. 26" by 38". Designed by Jane McGown Flynn.
"Hooked for my father, Oscar Traweek."

Crest. Hooked by Michele Micarelli, New Haven, Connecticut. 15" diameter. Designed by Jane McGown Flynn.
"My first Teacher's Workshop project. An altered Flynn pattern."

Mic-Cal. Designed and hooked by Michele Micarelli, New Haven, Connecticut. 28" by 32".
"My daughter-in-law's dachshund. He was a dog with a big attitude and lots of opinions."

Foot Stool. Hooked by Michele Micarelli, New Haven, Connecticut. 12" by 16". Designed by Pearl K. McGown. *Courtesy of Frank and Hart Caparulo.*
"A Christmas gift to Frank and Hart Caparulo, my brother and sister-in-law."

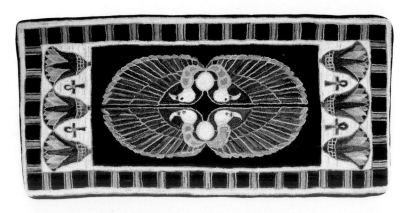

Osiris. Hooked by Michele Micarelli, New Haven, Connecticut. 22" by 28". Designed by Jane McGown Flynn.
"A McGown Teacher's Workshop project, colors inspired by the inlaid jewels of Egyptian artifacts."

Pansy Dreams. Hooked by Michele Micarelli, New Haven, Connecticut. 50" by 36". Designed by Charlotte Stratton.

"Had I named this rug, I would have called it 'The Great Pansy Wars.' It reminded me of my mother's adoration for these sweet flowers. It also reminded me of my parents' inability to communicate. My father was raised on a farm and turned our yard into a mini farm garden. Every edge of the yard was planted with pansies for my mother. She could see the garden from the window over the kitchen sink. Like all good farmers, my father was up with the birds, harvesting, hoeing, staking, and deadheading every open pansy and dropping them onto the flower bed. Later, when my mom did the breakfast dishes, she would see all the pansies lying there. She would run out and pick them all up and put them into tiny vases on all the windowsills. By the end of the day the pansies would be in full bloom again, only to have the scenario play out over and over all summer. I hooked this rug with the help of a masterful flower artist, Helen Connelly. I also wish to note here that I hooked this rug on old burlap that had to be patched several times while I was hooking it. This is a lesson I only had to learn once."

Holiday Purse. Designed and hooked by Michele Micarelli, New Haven, Connecticut. 14" by 12".
"A fun project with mixed materials and techniques, started in a class with Abby Vakay."

Spring Fever. Hooked by Michele Micarelli, New Haven, Connecticut. 45" by 68". Designed by Jane McGown Flynn.
"Hooked especially for a McGown Teacher's Workshop. The class I taught was called 'Flowers With No Swatches.'"

Gorilla. Designed and hooked by Michele Micarelli, New Haven, Connecticut. 22" by 18".

"I designed and hooked this gorilla portrait especially for a class at McGown Teacher's Workshop when the subject was 'hairy animals.' I have a special fondness for these animals. I belong to several gorilla conservation societies. One of my philosophies is, 'hook what you love and are familiar with.' Another philosophy I have, and perhaps the most important one is, 'look and see, really see, looking with observation and study in mind. Look carefully, because in order to hook something with a large amount of fine details, you will have to have very good visual aids and models, and look at them inch by inch.' I often go to the zoo to observe these animals. I have photos, books, and artwork with gorillas as the subject. My 'Gorilla' is currently available as a pattern from The House of Price, Inc."

"Another philosophy I have, and perhaps the most important one is, 'look and see, really see, looking with observation and study in mind. Look carefully, because in order to hook something with a large amount of fine details, you will have to have very good visual aids and models, and look at them inch by inch.' "

—Michele Micarelli

Deep Woods. Designed and hooked by Michele Micarelli, New Haven, Connecticut. 18" by 74".

" 'Deep Woods' is based on my love of The Arts and Crafts Movement and squirrels."

Cotton's House. Hooked by Michele Micarelli, New Haven, Connecticut. 28" by 38". Designed by Michele Micarelli and Ralph Caparulo. "My father's childhood home in Tuscaloosa, Alabama. Drawn with the help of my brother, Ralph Caparulo."

Basque Fairy Tale. Designed and hooked by Michele Micarelli, New Haven, Connecticut. 24" by 74".
"I was long into my adulthood when I began to communicate with some of my cousins who lived in the west. My mom had been an orphan and many details of our Spanish heritage had been lost. My cousins were caught up in the craze of finding ancestors and developing a family tree. It was at that time that they discovered we were of Basque descent. We read Basque history, ate Basque food, and enjoyed Basque fairy tales. While reading a fairy tale book, I noticed how detailed and beautiful the bookplates were at the beginning of each chapter. These were the inspiration for this rug."

Swamp Purse. Designed and hooked by Michele Micarelli, New Haven, Connecticut. 8" by 15". *Courtesy of Caroline LaMorte.*
"Mixed materials and techniques."

Chapter 2

2006 Green Mountain Rug Hooking Guild Honoree – Emily K. Robertson

The Green Mountain Rug Hooking Guild is delighted to honor Emily K. Robertson for her contribution to the field of rug hooking. Along with fellow honorees Pat Merikallio and Michele Micarelli, Emily was asked to show a body of her work at this year's exhibition. The following twenty-one rugs show her fascination with the craft and her ability to capture a glimpse of the world as seen through her keen eyes. She has a recognizable style all her own, and has found a way to turn soft sheep's wool into stunning light and shadow. In demand as a rug hooking teacher, she is well-known for her workshops, many of which focus on humor in hooked rugs.

Emily is a self-taught fiber artist who took up rug hooking fourteen years ago after a career in academic administration. She holds an undergraduate degree in art education as well as three advanced degrees in adult education, administration, and theology. She lives and believes in the maxim that "life is a continuing education."

Her interest in rug hooking as a medium stems from the freedom of expression it affords. She does not feel that she has made her best piece as of yet. Emily's work has been exhibited all over this country as well as in England in juried and non-juried shows. These include the Wenham Museum, the Hartford Athenaeum, and the Cahoon Museum. She has been the recipient of Sauder Village's "Best in Show" and the "Sauder Village" award. Her work has been featured in *Fiberarts Design Book Five*, *Fiberarts Design Book Seven*, *Folk Art* Magazine, *Rug Hooking* Magazine, and numerous books and newspaper articles including a feature in the *Boston Globe Sunday Magazine*.

She is a past board member of the Association of Traditional Hooking Artists, past president of the Cream City Rug Hookers Guild, and past program chair for the Cranberry Guild on Cape Cod, of which she is a member. She is also a member of the Green Mountain Rug Hooking Guild and serves on the Editorial Board at *Rug Hooking* Magazine. She provided the "Two of Spades" as part of the ongoing "Art of Playing Cards" exhibit.

In 2006, in addition to being an honoree at the Hooked in the Mountains XI show, Emily also had a one-woman show at Sherrill Library at the Episcopal Divinity School in Cambridge, Massachusetts, and was in the show "Folks in Fiber" at the Cahoon Museum on Cape Cod.

Emily has spent much of her fiber arts career doing commission work and her pieces are in private collections across this country and in England.

A Few Words From Emily

"I came to traditional rug hooking as the means of my artistic expression through researching various crafts. I find that the pulling up of loops of wool fabric through a backing upon which I have drawn my design allows me to freely express myself and to continue to grow in my artistic expression. The richness of color on wool never fails to excite and inspire me. I dye much of the fabric I use in my work, but also purchase already dyed fabric as well as recycling wool clothes found in thrift stores."

"Humor is a strong element in my work and I like to letter messages on my rugs that will make the viewer smile. The balance between intellect and sensuality is interesting and I hope that the viewer of my work will feel the effects of both."

"I started hooking under the name of Emily Erickson, but then nine years ago I met and married Mike Robertson, who is the love of my life. One of the biggest strengths of our marriage is that neither of us has any idea where or what we will be doing in five years, or in one year for that matter. It keeps our life open to possibilities and continually fresh. I have just completed my third advanced academic degree, this one in theology, and may very well become an ordained minister in the Congregational Church before the end of the year. Who knows? I have two children who are in their thirties, married, and living in Wisconsin where I lived most of my life. I also have two wonderful grandchildren, Abby and Alek."

"Mike and I went to hear Jane Fonda speak recently and she had a quote that is something for me to keep in mind: 'It is more important to be interested than to be interesting.' "

"I find that the pulling up of loops of wool fabric through a backing upon which I have drawn my design allows me to freely express myself and to continue to grow in my artistic expression. The richness of color on wool never fails to excite and inspire me."

—Emily K. Robertson

A hand painted sign for Emily Robertson's striking exhibit at the rug show. Painted by Rae Harrell.

Green Mountain Rug Hooking Guild Honoree Emily K. Robertson from Falmouth, Massachusetts is pictured here at the opening reception of Hooked in the Mountains XI. The reception was held at Shelburne Museum's historic Round Barn on March 31, 2006.

Window On Spring. Designed and hooked by Emily K. Robertson, Falmouth, Massachusetts. 62" by 36".
"An art gallery in Door County, Wisconsin was displaying my rugs for me. As I was delivering my work to the gallery I happened to look out the window, and there was the very image that you are looking at right now. It was so beautiful that I had to go home and hook it myself."

Serenity. Designed and hooked by Emily K. Robertson, Falmouth, Massachusetts. 55" by 33".
"This is a self-taught prodded piece that I made in 1998. It was made on a floor stand for hooking rugs. I never saw the front of it until it was finished and I could cut it off the stand and turn it over. I especially like the depth of image that is achieved through the use of wide and long pieces of wool."

Chelsea Garden. Designed and hooked by Emily K. Robertson, Falmouth, Massachusetts. 54" by 36".
"This rug was made about three years after I began rug hooking. It depicts the kind of garden found in New York City. I had fun working with a very limited palette and using 'as is' wool."

The Little Fairies. Designed and hooked by Emily K. Robertson, Falmouth, Massachusetts. 52" by 35".
"Many of my students have heard me tell them to finish their work because the little fairies will never come and do it for them. Imagine my surprise when I entered my studio one morning and found that I had been wrong. At least in one case, the little fairies actually had come to finish a rug!"

In England's Green and Pleasant Land. Designed and hooked by Emily K. Robertson, Falmouth, Massachusetts. 39" by 43".
"The building that is the focal point of this rug is the music department of Durham University in England. I had thought it to be a Manor House, but was mistaken. Where I have a flowery garden there is actually a cemetery. However, such minor inconsistencies do not lessen the idyllic sense of peace and home that I wanted to convey."

English Garden. Designed and hooked by Emily K. Robertson, Falmouth, Massachusetts. 50" by 36".
"The idea for this rug came from the fact that I felt that I had not made a 'pretty' rug for quite some time. The house and tree are images from Oxton, England where I was visiting Cilla Cameron. I hooked these elements first and the rug really looked like 'Bleak House!' However, after adding the flowers it became quite pretty, didn't it?"

A Friend in a Friend's Garden. Designed and hooked by Emily K. Robertson, Falmouth, Massachusetts. 48" by 60".
"A few years ago, while I was staying at a friend's home in a little village outside of Cambridge, England, my friend, Sarah Mustoe, took me on a walk through the village and into her friend's garden which was completely shut off from the road. It was a lovely and breathtaking experience to actually visit such a formal and beautiful garden as this one is."

Wisconsin Farm. Designed and hooked by Emily K. Robertson, Falmouth, Massachusetts. 48" by 60".
"This is an early rug in my career. I have spent most of my life in Wisconsin, and this rug exemplifies what Wisconsin is about. The beauty of the cultivated land and the order of the outbuildings is a composition in its own right."

Betsy. Designed and hooked by Emily K.
Robertson, Falmouth, Massachusetts. 23"
by 20".
"Betsy has been the best friend a rug hooker could have. When she was only a puppy
she became my quality control specialist.
No rug I ever made was complete unless
she sat on it. She has consistently approved
of my artistic and professional decisions.
This has been very encouraging for me."

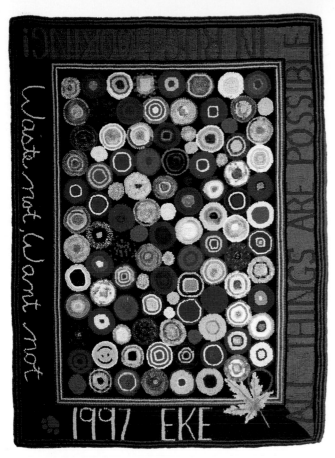

"The only problem with this technique is that while you think that you can use up all your scraps, it turns out that that is impossible! Leftover wool becomes a fact of life."
—Emily K. Robertson

Dog Paw Rug. Designed and hooked by Emily K. Robertson, Falmouth, Massachusetts. 50" by 36".
"This is my version of a cat's paw rug. Since I am a dog lover, I renamed the technique to suit my preference. The only problem with this technique is that while you think that you can use up all your scraps, it turns out that that is impossible! Leftover wool becomes a fact of life."

Abby. Designed and hooked by Emily K. Robertson, Falmouth, Massachusetts. 25" by 31".
"Abby is my granddaughter who lives in Wisconsin. The hat and dress she is wearing were her Easter outfit a few years ago. She is the apple of my eye."

English Tile Adaptation. Designed and hooked by Emily K. Robertson, Falmouth, Massachusetts. 32" by 17".
"I wanted to work with different values of complementary colors, and this tile pattern which I found in a Dover publication really worked well for my needs. The small rug covers a seat in my front hall and is the first hooked piece that a visitor sees as she enters my home."

The Rawls' Rug. Designed and hooked by Emily K. Robertson, Falmouth, Massachusetts. 144" by 34". *Courtesy of Bill and Penny Rawls, Camino Island, Washington.*

"This is a commission that I did in 2000. The clients are friends and they wanted a runner for their hallway depicting their family life. They love their Jack Russell terriers, who behave as though they are hooligans. I told them that if I was going to put so many of their misbehaving dogs into a rug, I would at least have one well behaved dog in it, too. This is why you can find my dog, Betsy, right in the middle. I am most pleased with the image of the horse and driver in the lower right corner."

Skip's House. Designed and hooked by Emily K. Robertson, Falmouth, Massachusetts. 38" by 37".
"For years, I avoided hooking an autumn colored rug because I thought that whenever I had tried, the results were trite. One day I looked out the window of my newly built studio and this image is what I saw. I worked and reworked the colors until I felt I had it 'right.' "

Faith of Our Mothers. Designed and hooked by Emily K. Robertson, Falmouth, Massachusetts. 47" by 50".
"It isn't often we get a blizzard on Cape Cod, but when we did a few years ago, I knew I had a perfect opportunity to work with a very limited color scheme and to see what I could do without my usual bright color palette. I wanted the house to fill one half of the rug while the trees and church took up the other half."

26

Falmouth Sunrise. Designed and hooked by Emily K. Robertson, Falmouth, Massachusetts. 10" by 17".
"I had some fun making this rug in the 'Grenfell Tradition' using dyed hosiery. The image is of my dog, Betsy, and me on the jetty at the harbor in Falmouth, Massachusetts where we live. As you can see from the rest of my work in the show, I don't usually work this small. It was very challenging for me to do so."

Celebration X. Designed and hooked by Emily K. Robertson, Falmouth, Massachusetts. 38" by 40".
"The year that I had the honor of being a judge for *Rug Hooking* magazine in the *Celebration* competition, along with Linda Rae Coughlin, Claire De Roos, and Jacalyn Krewson, I thought that it would be appropriate to hook a group portrait of us as judges. We were staying at a Day's Inn and the other wording just seemed to describe the event."

A Message About Grass. Designed and hooked by Emily K. Robertson, Falmouth, Massachusetts. 40" by 40".
"This is a message I had long wanted to hook into a rug. Last summer I finally had the opportunity. I wanted the hill to look 'David Hockney-ish,' reflecting back to the many happy times I have had with Heather Richie in North Yorkshire."

Reach for the Sky. Designed and hooked by Emily K. Robertson, Falmouth, Massachusetts. 64" by 42".
"Light and shadow have long been themes in my rugs. Before making this large rug, I had made a series of smaller ones concentrating on light coming through leaves. I wanted to try the same technique on a larger scale, and this is the result."

27

But, What About Us? Designed and hooked by Emily K. Robertson, Falmouth, Massachusetts. 47" by 27".

"I was given the challenge to make a Noah's Ark rug. After reading *The Bible* passages about this story I realized that nowhere are the plants ever mentioned. The whole story revolves around people and animals. So, what about the plants? What ever happened to them during the forty days and forty nights? Hmm."

Below:
We Are All Born in the Gutter… Designed and hooked by Emily K. Robertson, Falmouth, Massachusetts. 59" by 35".

"The quote around the edge of this rug is one of Oscar Wilde's. The night sky was drawn from nature one summer morning in Wisconsin. I am especially fond of this rug and of the saying on it. It hangs over the front door in my home. This is the first time I used the technique of swirling the sky, which you can see that I have done many times since."

28

Chapter 3
Animals

The animals listed in this chapter include dogs, horses, chickens, roosters, turkeys, rabbits, fish, reptiles, insects, and a variety of other wonderful beasts including, to name but a few, a moose, two pigs, a fox, a polar bear, a donkey, an elephant, a penguin, and several monkeys on snowboards. All other animals from the rug show (including cats, birds, sheep, cows, and wild animals) can be seen in this book's companion volume.

Dogs

Louky. Designed and hooked by Louise G. de Tonnancour, Brossard, Quebec, Canada. 29" by 39".
"Four years ago, Louky was a wonderful small puppy. I have enjoyed watching her grow into a beautiful mature dog full of energy. She is my walking companion and I love her dearly."

Love on the Run. Designed and hooked by Heidi Wulfraat, Lakeburn, New Brunswick, Canada. 53" by 27".
"This is my first hooked rug. It was designed in memory of my dear friend, 'Farmer,' who died one year ago at the age of fifteen. I like to believe that she still walks with me today."

Nugget and His Son. Hooked by Angelika H. Brumbaugh, Waitsfield, Vermont. 53" by 42". Designed by Nature.
"Nugget and his son were designed by Nature and recreated by me after my photograph."

Sharon's "MO". Designed and hooked by Kathleen Patten, Hinesburg, Vermont. 16" by 30".
"My good friend, Sharon Nimtz, said she hoped one day to have one of my original rugs, so I hooked this abstract of her standard poodle, 'MO.' "

Ginger. Designed and hooked by Joyce Combs, Lambertville, New Jersey. 25" by 29".
"My chocolate Labrador loves to hunt. This rug was started in a class with Elizabeth Black and then it took me several more years to complete the background."

Kallie's Brat Box. Designed and hooked by Kathy Hutchins, Cambridge, Vermont. 32" by 26".
"As a puppy, Kallie Belle watched anxiously the comings and goings of the world outside from her 'Brat Box.' Even as she lost her sight, she still continued to perch there. This rug depicts memories of a true friend."

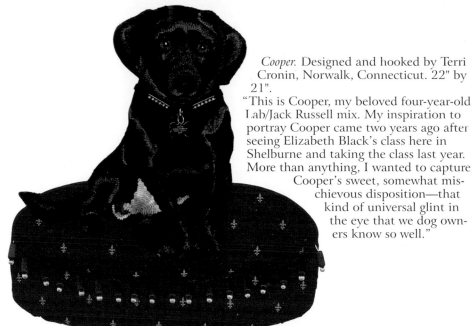

Cooper. Designed and hooked by Terri Cronin, Norwalk, Connecticut. 22" by 21".

"This is Cooper, my beloved four-year-old Lab/Jack Russell mix. My inspiration to portray Cooper came two years ago after seeing Elizabeth Black's class here in Shelburne and taking the class last year. More than anything, I wanted to capture Cooper's sweet, somewhat mischievous disposition—that kind of universal glint in the eye that we dog owners know so well."

I Loved Lucy. Designed and hooked by Shelley Poremski, Florence, Vermont. 18" by 17".

"When my three year old yellow Lab, Lucy, was killed in a tragic accident, I was heartbroken. I drew this picture of her and hooked it as a wall hanging to have as a daily reminder of her beauty and her undying devotion to me."

Adam's Dogs – Lake Tahoe. Designed and hooked by Layne G. Herschel, Chester, Vermont. 27" by 35".

"Adam, my son, lives near Lake Tahoe. His dogs Czar and Maki hike everywhere with him."

Loyal Friend. Designed and hooked by Dorothy Panaceck, Fredericksburg, Texas. 16" by 26".

"Inspiration for this rug came after having an 'Edward Frost Day' at my shop. We were lucky to have a number of old Frost rugs on display. I designed this rug to hook in Barb Carroll and Jule Marie Smith's 'Hannah' workshop."

Mavi. Hooked by Tricia Tague Miller, Alstead, New Hampshire. 23" by 36". Designed by Jacqueline Hansen of The 1840 House.

Sam and Casey. Hooked by Lisa Larrabee, Rome, Maine. 24" by 36". Designed by Elizabeth Black.
"As a new rug hooker of five months, I attended a workshop with Elizabeth Black, an artist and teacher who also drew this pattern. Sam and Casey are my Pekingese dogs. Sam is six years old and Casey is four months old in the rug. My rugs and dogs are my most precious possessions."

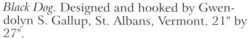

Mr. McDougall. Designed and hooked by Beverly Delnicki, Wheelock, Vermont. 19" by 21".
"From a photo of my dog—in a class with Jon Ciemiewicz at Geneva Point, October, 2005."

The Hodge. Designed and hooked by M. Kay Weeks, Port Murray, New Jersey. 23" by 36".
"A faithful companion of my son, 'The Hodge' was a German short haired pointer who left us in the spring. He was fourteen years old and we miss him greatly."

Black Dog. Designed and hooked by Gwendolyn S. Gallup, St. Albans, Vermont. 21" by 27".
"I designed 'Black Dog' for our dog Jessy; since she's a country dog, I wanted to portray her in primitive rug fashion."

Spot. Hooked by Arlene Jackman, Vergennes, Vermont. 29" by 43". Design adapted by Arlene Jackman from an original pattern by Joan Moshimer called "Putnam Historic."
"I have always loved this design and decided to modify it with a dog my daughter, Erin Jackman, had drawn in elementary school."

Lucy and Theo. Designed and hooked by Marilyn L. Sly, Mystic, Connecticut. 24" by 36".

Wild Corgi. Designed and hooked by Janet Williams, Skillman, New Jersey. 13" by 13".
"Exploring color and values in a portrait of my dog Winston, a Pembroke Welsh Corgi."

Bear. Hooked by Angelika H. Brumbaugh, Waitsfield, Vermont. 26" by 25". Designed by Nature.
"This stray dog appearing one day out of the woods found a loving home with my friend. Since I could not have him, I created him from a photograph for myself."

Yankee. Hooked by Margery Kimpton, Dunstable, Massachusetts. 36" by 45". Designed by Margery Kimpton with George Kahnle.
"Yankee is our grandson's 'golden doodle,' a golden retriever/poodle hybrid. The rug grew out of the April 2004 Green Mountain Rug Hooking Guild 'Design and Dye' workshop with George Kahnle and Dick LaBarge. I hope they are as pleased as Yankee and her boy are with the result."

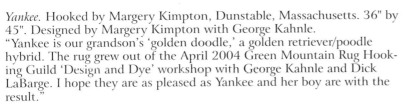

Patriotic Trio. Hooked by Ruth St. George, Shelburne, Vermont. 24" by 55". Designed by Nancy Urbanak of Beaver Brook Crafts.

"What I love about punch hooking and this mat is that they both are so joyful. The varied yarns and wools are just a happy experience."
—Suzanne Dirmaier

Lexie. Designed and hooked by Eunice Whitney Heinlein, Avon, Connecticut. 29" by 41".
"Lexie was rescued from the dog pound and shared our lives for six years."

Green Dog. Designed and hooked by Judy Quintman, Wilmington, North Carolina. 19" by 25".
"I was experimenting with different backgrounds and decided to use up a bunch of scraps of greens."

Clemintine. Designed and hooked by Suzanne Dirmaier, Waterbury Center, Vermont. 13" by 13".
"I took Amy Oxford's punch hooking class last year and created this as my first piece. What I love about punch hooking and this mat is that they both are so joyful. The varied yarns and wools are just a happy experience."

Airedale. Hooked by Jeni Nunnally, Cape Neddick, Maine. 24" by 34". Designed by Polly Minick.
"I started this rug at Marion Ham's rug camp and finished it with Sarah Guiliani. The design reminded me of a dog I loved once."

Sam. Designed and hooked by Susie Stephenson, Edgecomb, Maine. 55" by 36".
"This is my dog, Sam, on squares of recycled wool left over from other projects. His tail is wool roving."

Horses

Whirligig. Hooked by Melonie Bushey, Vergennes, Vermont. 25" by 36". Designed by Beverly Conway Designs.

Whirligig. Hooked by Jane Perry, Shelburne, Vermont. 24" by 35". Designed by Beverly Conway Designs.
"A wonderful color workshop weekend was spent sitting on the lawn in South Hero hooking, drinking lemonade, and color planning with Bev Conway. She gets 95% of the credit for the colors in 'Whirligig' and 100% credit for the design!"

Braeside Farm. Designed and hooked by Jay McGarry, Chittenden, Vermont. 37" by 59".
"This rug represents my love of 'Eventing,' which is a triathlon-like horse show! It includes dressage, stadium jumping, and cross country jumping. This is my first real rug. Thank you Kathy Hutchins for all your wonderful input."

Draft Horse. Hooked by Karen Detrick, New Lexington, Ohio. 22" by 28". Designed by Woolie Delight.

Untitled. Hooked by Eleanor de Vecchis, Cutchogue, New York. 25" by 30".

Welcome Home. Designed and hooked by Debi Price, Colchester, Vermont. 14" by 25". "Inspired by my friend's love of horses and how welcome she makes me feel at her home."

Magdalena's Double Horses. Hooked by Davey DeGraff, Hinesburg, Vermont. 24" by 42". Designed by Woolley Fox LLC/Barb Carroll.

Running Horse. Designed and hooked by Sue Hammond, New London, New Hampshire. 28" by 34". "The horse design is taken from an old weather vane."

Let Me Out! Designed and hooked by Tracy Jamar, New York, New York. 14" by 15".

Lillie Day and Ladeda. Designed and hooked by Eugenie Delaney, North Ferrisburgh, Vermont.
29" by 23".
"Lillie and Lade belong to my friend Lynda Malzac. I hooked this rug for her in gratitude for all the help and support she gives me with the equine members of my family."

WEE SASS
TWICE BOLD   WEE NATIVE

Krista B. Designed and hooked by Gail Majauckas, West Newbury, Massachusetts. 17" by 12".
"A favorite horse who spent over twenty years with us, Krista B is hooked with a variety of dark
colors, greens, blues, and purples in #4 cut to achieve her dark color. The frame is made from
boards from her paddock fence, complete with her teeth marks. Teacher, Elizabeth Black's expertise at Shelburne, 2005, was indispensable."

Eve's Stone Barn. Designed and hooked by Barbara Lukas, Ottawa, Ontario, Canada. 24" by 19". "With thanks to Eve Mainwaring for her generosity in teaching Loulou the meaning of sportsmanship and life."

Dobbin. Hooked by Rebecca L. Cridler, Charles Town, West Virginia. 28" by 43". Designed by Lib Callaway. "From a love of horses. You can never have too many."

"My son, Braeden, asked me to hook a rug with a horse riding a cowboy. So I did! The horse is my son's pony, 'Frost on the Pumpkin,' aka Punky. This rug represents Punky's true personality."

—Jay McGarry

Save a Horse, Ride a Cowboy. Designed and hooked by Jay McGarry, Chittenden, Vermont. 33" by 24". "My son, Braeden, asked me to hook a rug with a horse riding a cowboy. So I did! The horse is my son's pony, 'Frost on the Pumpkin,' aka Punky. This rug represents Punky's true personality."

Three Doodle Doos. Hooked by Susan Gingras, Weybridge, Vermont. 47" by 21". Designed by Vermont Folk Rugs.

Wake Up. Designed and hooked by Jean Brinegar, Mt. Holly, Vermont. 24" by 32".
"I developed this design from my love of and constant amusement with chickens. They are ever inspirational."

Chicken Soup. Hooked by Janet C. Berner, South Newfane, Vermont. 17" by 22". Designed by Yankee Peddler.

Border Series #6 – Rooster. Designed and hooked by Judy Quintman, Wilmington, North Carolina. 30" by 31".
"I saw a napkin with a cute rooster on it. So, I thought a rooster (my own version) would make a good center for my border series."

Rise and Shine. Designed and hooked by Cynthia Shepard, Grand Isle, Vermont. 17" by 22". "This is my first rug. Sandra Ashley, DonnaSue Shaw, and Missy VanMarter-Rexford encouraged me to try rug hooking and join this guild. I started with a rooster because I like them and then chose the elements in my background to add depth and interest to my design."

Strawberry Bandit. Hooked by Janet C. Berner, South Newfane, Vermont. 9" by 12". Designed by Fluff and Peachy Bean Designs.

Prize Roosters. Hooked by Susan Higley, Queensbury, New York. 27" by 63". Designed by George Kahnle for Hooked on the Creek.
"George Kahnle's patterns are so whimsical and fun. This pattern has everything I wanted to hook: people, birds, flowers, and an unusual border."

Big Hen. Designed and hooked by Karen Detrick, New Lexington, Ohio. 24" by 30". "Inspired by a quote from my Mom. When she arrived home from work she announced 'The big hen's on the roost.' The irony is she was only five feet tall."

Top of the Morning. Hooked by Pamela Anfuso, Milford, New Hampshire. 30" by 30". Designed by Jane McGown Flynn.

Wake Up Call. Hooked by Karen Martin, Burlington, Vermont. 26" by 33". Designed by Karen Martin with rooster drawn by Jon Ciemiewicz.
"This rug was finished during the time my husband was recovering from quadruple bypass surgery. His experience sure was a wake up call for us."

Rufus. Hooked by Judith Latour, Granby, Massachusetts. 22" by 22". Designed by Woolley Fox LLC/Barb Carroll.

Morning Call. Hooked by Mary Pringle, South Hero, Vermont. 25" by 35". Designed by Eugenie Delaney for Beverly Conway Designs.

Top of The Morning (Adaptation). Hooked by Darcy Cardas, Bandon, Oregon. 25" by 30". Designed by Jane McGown Flynn.
"As a term of endearment, my husband refers to me as a Spring Chicken, so I call him The Cocky Rooster. This rug is for his stereo room."

Running Rooster. Hooked by Theresa Boise, Middlebury, Vermont. 17" by 31". Designed by Sally Kallin, Pine Island Primitives.

"This rooster brought back childhood memories of a rooster we had on our family farm. He used to chase me and my brothers and sister when we were anywhere near him."

Gobble. Designed and hooked by Joanna Henderson, Hopkinton, New Hampshire. 23" by 40".

Bob's Turkey. Hooked by Robin H. Falta, Cornwall, Vermont. 23" by 31". Designed by Barb Kaiser.

"My husband repeatedly asked me to hook a turkey rug for him and I kept putting him off. My friend drew this pattern for me and I secretly hooked it last year, finishing (of course) on Christmas Eve. He still can't believe I hooked it without him knowing, and it is now his favorite rug."

Hit or Miss Weathercock. Hooked by Sue Ryan, Lyme, New Hampshire. 19" by 31". Designed by DiFranza Designs.

Flower Rooster. Hooked by Mary Hulette, South Burlington, Vermont. 26" by 37". Designed by Lib Calloway.

"This was a wedding present for Eric and Jane Yates. I have known Eric since he was a small child when his mom, Maureen, became my friend. Eric and Jane were married in Bend, Oregon on March 19, 2005 and now live in Eugene, Oregon, where they both are lawyers."

*"This rug was inspired by the daily scene
in our barnyard. Before completion, it became
a memorial rug—a small red fox ran off with
both subjects."*

—*Judith English*

Cornwall Free Range. Designed and hooked by Judith English, Cornwall, Vermont. 25" by 54".
"This rug was inspired by the daily scene in our barnyard. Before completion, it became a memorial rug—
a small red fox ran off with both subjects. I used a combination of 'as is' and overdyed wool, size 8 cut."

Hannah's Hens

In April 2005, Barbara Carroll from the company Woolley Fox, located in Pennsylvania, came to Shelburne to teach a mini workshop. The class was called "Hannah's Hen," and participants worked on Barb's charming pattern of the same name. Some of the students displayed their rugs at this year's exhibit and show-goers enjoyed seeing how each rug was modified and embellished.

Hannah's Hen. Hooked by Ginger Selman, West Newbury, Massachusetts. 20" by 27". Designed by Woolley Fox LLC/Barb Carroll.
"A special class last year at Shelburne. I added a border of eggs and a 'baby' peeping out of an egg. Barbara had a wonderful class to inspire your imagination."

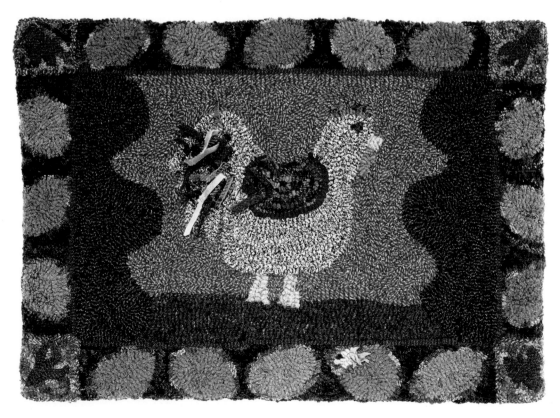

Hannah's Hen. Hooked by Elizabeth M. Edwards, Williston, Vermont. 22" by 16". Designed by Woolley Fox LLC/Barb Carroll.

Hannah's Hen. Hooked by Karen Doliber, West Newbury, Massachusetts. 21" by 29". Designed by Woolley Fox LLC/Barb Carroll.
"This fun project was the result of Barbara Carroll's mini workshop last April. I added the border to extend the colors of the center of the rug."

Hannah's Hen. Hooked by Karen Quigley, Vergennes, Vermont. 16" by 23". Designed by Woolley Fox LLC/Barb Carroll.
"From a 2005 workshop at Shelburne taught by Barbara Carroll."

48

Crazy Eggs from Hannah's Hen. Hooked by Nancy E. Baker, Shelburne, Vermont. 14" by 26". Designed by Woolley Fox LLC/Barb Carroll.
" 'Crazy Eggs' is a modification of Barbara Carroll's 'Hannah's Hen.' To make the design more lively and colorful, I added Hannah laying crazy eggs, which is a play on the game 'Crazy Eights.' "

Hannah's Blue Hen. Hooked by Cheryl Connor, Bridport, Vermont. 15" by 17". Designed by Woolley Fox LLC/Barb Carroll.
"Last year at the rug show in Shelburne, I took a fun-filled course from Barbara Carroll called 'Hannah's Hen.' I decided to hook a blue hen with a colorful tail of wool strips. The rug is hooked using traditional wool strips and I punched the black background with yarn. This is another chair pad for my dining room chairs."

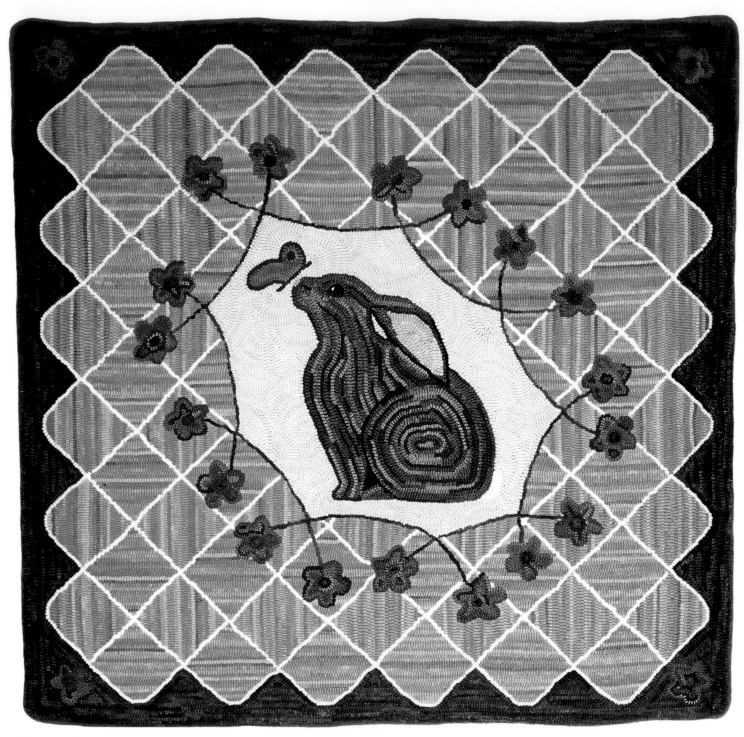

Enchanted. Designed and hooked by Leslie Goldring, Ferrisburg, Vermont. 41" by 41".
"My kids and I recently moved to a house with a few acres of fields. We were delighted to discover we share the property with the cutest little brown bunnies."

Horatio. Designed and hooked by Linda Repasky, Amherst, Massachusetts. 9" by 14".

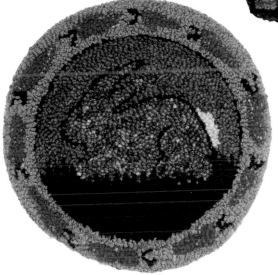

Ring Around the Bunny. Hooked by Karen Quigley, Vergennes, Vermont. 15" diameter. Designed by Breezy Ridge Rugs.

Rocky Mountain Hare. Hooked by Dee Rosebrock, Lawrenceville, New Jersey. 17" by 26". Design adapted by Dee Rosebrock from a John James Audubon lithograph dated 1848.

"In 2004, I began rug hooking lessons with Claudia Casebolt. Claudia showed me how to adapt one of my favorite John James Audubon lithographs into a rug. This is my first rug and it incorporates two things I love—the Rocky Mountains and rabbits."

Leaping Rabbit. Hooked by Kathy Boozan, South Burlington, Vermont. 36" by 27". Design adapted by Kathy Boozan from original artwork by Robyn Pandolph.

"Inspiration for my rug came from a quilt pattern, 'Seasons of the Heart' designed by Robyn Pandolph. I adapted the pattern to fit my piece of burlap, and added my own border. I used primary colors and recycled wool. The blue color was dyed by Bobbi Pond."

Magnum Opus. Hooked by Signa L. Read, Peru, Vermont. 55" by 60". Design adapted by Signa Read from the artwork of Ando Hiroshige.
"The source of my design is the 'Akodai' painting of the red rockfish by Japanese artist Ando Hiroshige (1797-1858)."

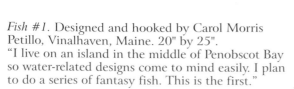

Fish #1. Designed and hooked by Carol Morris Petillo, Vinalhaven, Maine. 20" by 25".
"I live on an island in the middle of Penobscot Bay so water-related designs come to mind easily. I plan to do a series of fantasy fish. This is the first."

Coral Reef. Hooked by Denise W. Jose, Keuka Park, New York. 16" by 26". Designed by Jon Ciemiewicz.

The Slipperiest Thing in the World. Designed and hooked by Susan Alain, Montreal, Quebec, Canada. 37" by 54". "My friend Charlie Finck (a fisherman), asked me, 'What is the slipperiest thing in the world?' This is the reply and I hooked it in his handwriting."

Jellyfish. Hooked by Denise W. Jose, Keuka Park, New York. 20" by 12". Designed by Jon Ciemiewicz.

Kiss the Cod – Goodbye. Designed and hooked by Judith Dallegret, Montreal, Quebec, Canada. 36" by 52". "This is a rug to the mighty cod fish, which is fast disappearing from our oceans."

53

"Turtles are special to me—they remind us to slow down, to have patience, and to know that everything we need is within us. This is my first rug—I love rug hooking."

—Clearwater Liberty

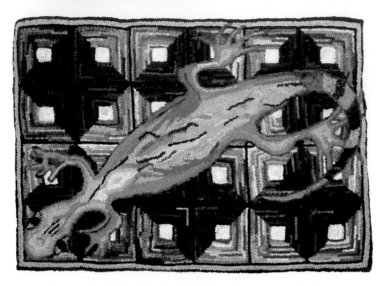

Lizard on Log Cabin. Hooked by Brenda Williams, Valatie, New York. 27" by 39". Designed by Gail Dufresne.

Dance of the Turtles. Designed and hooked by Clearwater Liberty, Wendell, Massachusetts. 22" by 32".
"Turtles are special to me—they remind us to slow down, to have patience, and to know that everything we need is within us. This is my first rug—I love rug hooking."

Walking Stick. Designed and hooked by Cheryl Raywood, Westport, New York. 15" by 22". Design adapted by Cheryl Raywood from a botanical illustration.

Silkmoth. Designed and hooked by Cheryl Raywood, Westport, New York. 14" by 20". Design adapted by Cheryl Raywood from a botanical illustration.

Millennium Bugs. Designed and hooked by Sarah McNamara, Greenport, New York. 15" by 42".
" 'Millennium Bugs' was my entry in a challenge issued by my guild for its rug show in 2000. The Y2K bug was all anyone talked about then, so I decided to play off that phrase. I drew actual bugs, but hooked them in bright colors and embellished them with a variety of sparkly stuff."

Monarchollage. Designed and hooked by Kathleen Menzies, Greenfield Park, Quebec, Canada. 23" by 31".
"This was my first rug. The design was inspired by a project I was working on with my kindergarten students, during which we observed and sketched the life cycle of butterflies. I experimented with dyes, marbleizing, 'as is' fabrics, and yarn."

Grenfell With Polar Bear Relief. Hooked by Maureen Rowe, Dollard-Des-Ormeaux, Quebec, Canada. 12" by 15". Designed by Rittermere-Hurst-Field.
"I wanted to honor the Grenfell tradition by hooking with my favorite bear, the Canada goose, some mountains, and glacier ice in the arctic."

Grasshopper #1. Designed and hooked by Robin Wilson, Ridgefield, Connecticut. 19" by 54".
" 'Grasshopper #1' came to life in Jayne Hester's summer class. The image is from a weathervane and the color palette was designed to 'get me out of the box.' The ferns are designed to recreate a shadowing effect that I like in old rugs."

Be a Penguin. Designed and hooked by Shelley Poremski, Florence, Vermont. 12" by 17".
"After seeing the movie *March of the Penguins*, my daughter Hilary was deeply impressed by the tenacity of these amazing animals. Working full-time and going to school as well was taking a toll on her. I punch hooked this wall hanging as a reminder of her inner strength and determination."

A Tribute to My Grandmother. Designed and hooked by Barbara Kaiser, Cornwall, Vermont. 24" by 48".
"Originally my rug was to be an elephant rug hooked in my grandmother's memory; this was her favorite animal. The year that I started designing it, I wanted to purchase a mule. My husband and I were also arguing about the upcoming election, hence the flag; hence the finished rug!"

Moose Berries. Designed and hooked by Patricia Lawrence, Randolph, Vermont. 24" by 37".
"I used two favorite things, moose and strawberries, in the design of this punch needle rug. My husband and daughter helped to draw the moose. The border, with three intertwining yarns, was a new challenge."

Solitude. Hooked by Delma Schoeppler, Wallingford, Vermont. 24" by 36". Designed by Jane McGown Flynn.
"My love of animals and the help of my teacher and friend Elizabeth Morgan."

Leaping Deer. Hooked by Susan Higley, Queensbury, New York. 34" by 51". Designed by George Kahnle for Hooked on the Creek.
"I love the simplicity of this pattern. When I found the wool 'blue stew' for the background, I knew I had to use it in this piece."

Starry Night. Hooked by Karen Quigley, Vergennes, Vermont. 16" by 23". Designed by Kris Miller/ Spruce Ridge Studios.
"Simply stated design in a primitive style. Few colors enhance the style of this design."

56

Irish Pig. Hooked by Carole Picard, Newburgh, New York. 25" by 42". Designed by Jane McGown Flynn.

The Uninvited Guest. Designed and hooked by Rickey Poor, Cornish, New Hampshire. 20" by 26".

"I started this rug in Emmy Robertson's 'Humor in Rugs' class. As a gardener, I have been fighting woodchucks for years. Just when my lettuces are ready for the first picking, or the broccoli and carrots are really getting started, my uninvited dinner guest inevitably comes and helps himself."

Beauty and the Beast. Designed and hooked by Bonnie Hancock Miller, New York, New York. 29" by 44".

Fall Folk Art Collage. Hooked by Lois Johnstone, Wallingford, Vermont. 25" by 33". Design adapted by Lois Johnstone from the Pearl McGown pattern "Maple Rhythm."

"I found this Pearl McGown pattern in a thrift store. It had been partly hooked by an unknown rug hooker. I loved it so I salvaged it. It was very large and I didn't want to finish the whole thing. My friend Sandy Marquis said, 'Why don't you just cut off the piece you want?' So I did, and I added the squirrel which was drawn by Claire Bornarth. I completed the hooking and then added the braided border."

Prairie Fox. Hooked by Carole Picard, Newburgh, New York. 26" by 53". Designed by Kathy Morton.

Squirrel. Hooked by Elizabeth Morgan, Wallingford, Vermont. 15" diameter. Designed by Nancy Urbanak of Beaver Brook Crafts.

Noah's Ark. Hooked by Sandi Goldring, Essex Junction, Vermont. 30" by 44". Designer unknown.

The Ark. Hooked by Rita Chabre, Brattleboro, Vermont. 17" by 20". Designed by Woolley Fox LLC/Barb Carroll.

58

Hot Doggin'. Designed and hooked by Tricia Tague Miller, Alstead, New Hampshire. 22" by 34".

Monkeys on Snowboards. Designed and hooked by Betty Bouchard, Richmond, Vermont. 22" by 25".

"This rug commemorates the birth of my youngest grandchild. His parents are avid snowboarders and his room is decorated with monkeys."

Harvest Moon. Hooked by Karen Detrick, New Lexington, Ohio. 34" by 45". Design taken from original artwork by Susan Winget.
"Adapted with permission from a September 2002 Farmhouse Wall Calendar."

Top Heavy. Hooked by Melonie Bushey, Vergennes, Vermont. 40" by 21". Designed by Vermont Folk Rugs.

The Mill Cat's Tale – in memoriam cat mats for cats to lie on. Designed and hooked by Ann Hallett, Coldwater, Ontario, Lokieo, Canada. 76" by 16".
"Coldwater, Ontario, like many villages, has many discarded, abandoned, disposable cats. They seemed to congregate at the Grist Mill. This was a problem. Some kindly townspeople, under cover of darkness, fed the stray cats. This was also a problem. 'The cats must go' said the Coldwater Mill Heritage Committee!"

My Animals. Designed and
hooked by Sherry M. Sollace,
Alburg, Vermont. 36" by 42".

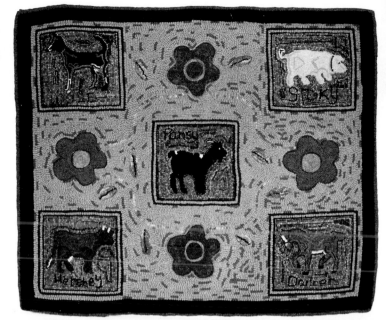

Friends. Designed and hooked by Debi Price, Colchester, Vermont. 14" by 26".
"Inspired by friendship quilts, I designed this for my friend Patty. The green hills and blue sky on the side represent our hikes in the Green Mountains of Ripton, Vermont."

Kerman Caravan. Hooked by Maureen Towner, Vancouver, Washington.
25" by 38". Designed by Jane McGown Flynn.

Keagan's Kat. Hooked by Mary I. Jameson, Brattleboro, Vermont. 22" by 28". Rug by Mary I. Jameson is based on the "House Cat" pattern found in *Rug Hooking For The First Time® by Donna Lovelady,* ©2003 by Donna Lovelady, a Sterling/Chapelle book, and is reprinted with permission of Sterling Publishing Co., Inc. "My granddaughter, Keagan, has a black cat named Mulligan. Mulligan is famous for having survived being lost for ten days, only to discover that he was in 'Grandma's' garage all that time. We think the garage door scared him."

Tumbling Cats. Hooked by Judith Hettesheimer, Hudson, New York. 35" by 52". Designed by Dahlov Ipcar.
"Adapted from the pattern 'Tumbling Cats' found in the book *Hooked Rugs* by Ann Davies and Emma Tennant."

Tapestry Animals. Hooked by Barbara Holt Hussey, Hinsdale, New Hampshire. 23" by 20". Designed by DiFranza Designs.

Tumbling Cats. Hooked by Nancy Z. Parcels, Mechanicsburg, Pennsylvania. 37" by 59". Designed by Dahlov Ipcar.
"This rug is featured in the book *Hooked Rugs* by Ann Davies and Emma Tennant. It evokes the work of Henri 'Le Douanier' Rousseau. I used over a hundred different hand dyed wools in this piece. There is also one piece of antique paisley from my dear friend and mentor, Yvonne Miller."

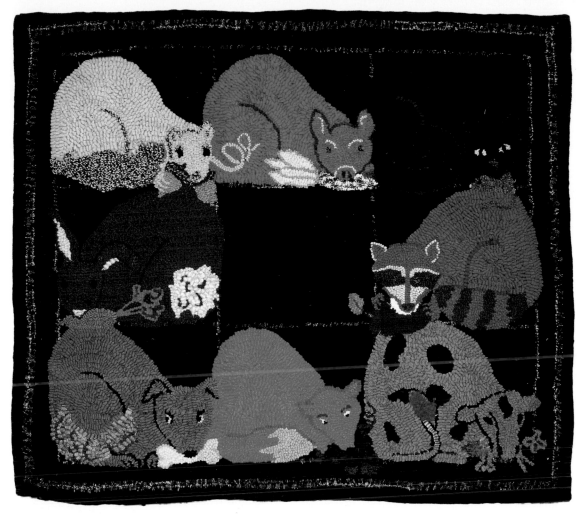

Faux Fauve. Designed and hooked by Barbara Holt Hussey, Hinsdale, New Hampshire. 28" by 32".
" 'Faux Fauve' is my first rug design. It was inspired by the brilliant Fauvist artist, Franz Marc. I am drawn to his work because of his use of saturated color and portrayal of animals."

Faux Fauve Fox Study #1. Designed and hooked by Barbara Holt Hussey, Hinsdale, New Hampshire. 10" by 12".

Faux Fauve Cat Study #2. Designed and hooked by Barbara Holt Hussey, Hinsdale, New Hampshire. 9" by 11".
"When I started hooking 'Faux Fauve' I realized I needed to capture the form and character in natural color before applying Fauvist color."

Chapter 4

People

Faces

Rug hooking classes, offered by our guild at the "Hooked in the Mountains" rug school, inspire and encourage students to try new things. Our members also teach classes all across the country and overseas. This year, instructors Rae Harrell, Anne-Marie Littenberg, and Diane Phillips have all taught workshops on different ways to hook the human face. One of the most well-represented subjects in the show, "Faces" has captured the guild's imagination. Many additional portraits can be seen in the "Strong Women" chapter of this book's companion volume.

"I don't know where this design came from—it just flowed out of me."
—*Donna Beaudoin*

Art. Designed and hooked by Donna Beaudoin, Hinesburg, Vermont. 26" by 16". "I don't know where this design came from—it just flowed out of me."

Robert (Strong Family I). Designed and hooked by Susan Alain, Montreal, Quebec, Canada. 20" by 16".
"Made in a 2005 'Faces' class with Diane Phillips."

Susan (Strong Family II). Designed and hooked by Susan Alain, Montreal, Quebec, Canada. 20" by 16".
"Started after doing a 'Faces' class with Diane Phillips in 2005. I am in the process of doing the whole family."

My Portrait. Designed and hooked by Bonnie LaPine, Essex Junction, Vermont. 20" by 16".
"Fantastic class given by Rae Harrell in 2005. Fun, faces, and friends. Who could ask for more?"

My Heart in My Hand. Designed and hooked by Tony Latham, Montreal, Quebec, Canada. 24" by 15".
"This design came out of a workshop with Rae Harrell. Inspiration for the piece came from a meditation on love, compassion, and an open heart."

In the Kingdom of Justice: Memorial For All Who Perished in New Orleans. Designed and hooked by Burma Cassidy, Rochester, Vermont. 19" by 20".
"I wanted to express my deep sadness over the tragedy of Hurricane Katrina. I used red, white, and blue to show the U.S. flag colors and lots of blue for the rising waters. The crown of thorns symbolizes the suffering."

Does It Resemble Me? Designed and hooked by Gail Du-clos Lapierre, Shelburne, Vermont. 17" diameter.
"Designed in a weekend workshop with Rae Harrell. After signing up for this class, I feared what I had gotten myself into, but I had a wonderful time! This was so outside the box for me, and it was great fun."

"Hands-On" Face. Hooked by Priscilla Heininger, Shelburne, Vermont. 21" by 17". Designed by Priscilla Heininger and Rae Harrell.
"Rae Harrell inspired and guided this piece in her 'hands-on' face class. We literally used our hands to measure and draw our faces instead of looking in mirrors or at photos. I appreciate Rae's guidance, encouragement, and artistic help in the outcome of this project!"

Othello. Hooked by Gloria Reynolds, Hines-burg, Vermont. 23" by 23". Design adapted by Gloria Reynolds from Shakespeare.
"*Othello*, like most of Shakespeare's plays, re-vealed man's inherent tendency to believe gossip and falsehoods. Alas! Othello smothered Desdemona, whose heart and love were chaste and pure. Remorsefully, before killing himself, Othello spoke thus: 'Speak of me as I am, one that loved not wisely, but too well.'"

Dr. Cheney. Designed and hooked by Jean E. MacQuiddy, Weston, Massachusetts. 24" by 36".

Favorites. Designed and hooked by Susan DeGregorio, Salem, New Hampshire. 19" by 22".
"Warm and cheerful sunshine, a budding tree in springtime, music, bird chirping outside my window, flowers, my cat Sabrina, and my family (their names are included in the background)."

The Colors of My Mind. Designed and hooked by Jill Cooper, Riverdale, Georgia. 41" by 27".
"In addition to rug hooking, I'm a folk art doll designer. During a face class with Rae Harrell, I discovered a way to show my love of both. The inset circle tells the story. I was able to leap out of the box with hooking as I had always done with my dolls."

Rigoletto. Designed and hooked by Burma Cassidy, Rochester, Vermont. 41" by 22". "Scene from Verdi's opera, *Rigoletto*."

Breaking New Ground. Designed and hooked by Janice Peyton, Excello, Missouri. 21" by 20".

Gardening. Hooked by Susan Gingras, Weybridge, Vermont. 37" by 22". Designed by Beverly Conway Designs.
"I hooked this rug for my sister-in-law, Jane. She is a superior gardener and a wonderful person!"

Avalon Dreams. Designed and hooked by Fran Hulette, Lawrenceville, New Jersey. 18" by 26".
"Inspiration for this rug came from the ambiance of Avalon, a New Jersey shore town I visit every summer, and from sea-themed art I've seen there."

Bubble Bath. Hooked by Priscilla Heininger, Shelburne, Vermont. 33" by 47". Designed by Beverly Conway Designs.
"This whimsical design by Beverly Conway makes me smile! I also appreciate her help in the color planning of this rug."

The Green Rug. Designed and hooked by Rachelle LeBlanc, Ste-Julie, Quebec, Canada. 32" by 28".
"My portrait. Inspired by me."

Blacksmith and Horseshoer Trade Sign. Hooked by Karl Gimber, Carversville, Pennsylvania. 27" by 29". Designed by Mary Jo Gimber.
"Inspired by an antique trade sign."

Molly McEgan. Designed and hooked by Susan DeGregorio, Salem, New Hampshire. 12" by 12".
"Challenged to create something in a 12" by 12" square, I came up with a little lady—Molly McEgan."

Summer of '45. Hooked by Willy Cochran, Jericho, Vermont. 20" by 16". Design adapted from an original photograph and drawn on linen by Roslyn Logsdon. "A wonderful memory of my husband and me when we were very young."

Below:
Buster Rides…By the Little Red House. Hooked by Nancy Z. Parcels, Mechanicsburg, Pennsylvania. 25" by 37". Design adapted by Nancy Z. Parcels from a pattern by Mildred Sprout.
"This rug was inspired by an antique Mildred Sprout pattern. My granddaughter named the boy Buster. The yellow roses were dyed using gathered goldenrod."

Nat's Delight. Hooked by Arlene Scanlon, Essex Junction, Vermont. 20" by 15". Design adapted by Roslyn Logsdon from a family photograph belonging to Arlene Scanlon. "The photo was a favorite of my Aunt Natalie. It is a picture of myself and my cousin Gene outside my grandparents' house in New Hampshire."

Please Let Me Call You. Hooked by Melonie Bushey, Vergennes, Vermont. 27" by 46". Designed by Beverly Conway Designs.

"Jesus Wept" – John 11:35. Designed and hooked by Paige Osborn Stoep, Lyons, New York. 9" by 25".

The Light of the Mind is Blue. Designed and hooked by Carol T. Dale, Gilford, New Hampshire. 30" by 32".
"Hooked with wools from my grandmother's stash. I adapted my design from an old Navaho rug, then added a line of poetry by Sylvia Plath written in the Runic alphabet."

Sarah and Coco. Designed and hooked by Ruth McLoughlin, Rochester, Vermont. 15" by 17".
"This was a memory piece done while studying with Cleland Selby. My daughter Sarah and our dog Coco were walking down Bingo Road in Rochester, Vermont."

Indian Chiefs. Designed and hooked by Carol T. Dale, Gilford, New Hampshire. 20" by 22".
"I designed this piece at a workshop with Roslyn Logsdon in Waitsfield, Vermont. The challenge was to make different textures and color plans work harmoniously in a small piece."

Emergence. Designed and hooked by Tricia Tague Miller, Alstead, New Hampshire. 25" by 36".
"This rug portrays the story of the Pueblo people's emergence from the underworld to this. One tale tells of how they followed Badger, who carried a fire stick to light the way. A long journey followed before they settled. Symbols tell the tale."

Apples. Designed and hooked by Rachelle LeBlanc, Ste-Julie, Quebec, Canada. 46" by 56".
"It was such a wonderful day. The sun was out and the green from the trees was wonderful. My two daughters, Lauren and Emanuelle, with their friend Magalie."

Relaxin' on a Sunday Afternoon. Designed and hooked by Janice E. Bogan, Clifton Park, New York. 37" by 25".

"Inspired by an old black and white picture from my mother's album showing my great-grandparents and either my grandfather or one of his brothers. I assume the picture was taken in the late 1800s or early 1900s in South Carolina. I imagine that 'back in the day,' when boys wore dresses and women smoked corncob pipes, after a week of hard labor, Sunday was the day to worship and relax."

Sarah's Dolls. Designed and hooked by Sarah Guiliani, South Portland, Maine. 34" by 38".
"I love this rug. The dolls are my own dolls I have at home."

Wedding Rug. Designed and hooked by Sherry Lowe, South Glastonbury, Connecticut. 31" by 55".
"I designed and punch hooked this rug as a wedding present for my son, Eric, and his wife, Katie. It incorporates many things that are special in their lives. The outhouse was for Katie who was in charge of sanitation in Bolivia in the Peace Corps. (People always ask!)"

Four Seasons. Designed and hooked by Janet Conner, Hiram, Maine. 45" by 46".

"This piece was inspired by an Elizabethan woodcut that always fascinated me. It was fun to imagine the little black and white image in an expanded size and color."

The Family Tree – Not One of Thee is Like Another – Don't Ask Me Why – Go Ask Your Mother! (From Dr. Seuss). Designed and hooked by Ann Hallett, Coldwater, Ontario, Lokieo, Canada. 40" by 57".

"Designed from the actual hand prints of three generations of my family. Eight of them are hookers, and hooked some of their own hands. A delightful bonus was being reunited with my nephew's talented artistic daughter, Echo, who had been estranged from us since she was three."

Reach High Clara. Designed and hooked by Joyce Combs, Lambertville, New Jersey. 19" by 40".

"Hooked with love for my first grandchild. Rug shows a tracing of her hands at one year old, reaching for the stars. Tracings of her father and fraternal grandparents on the right, and her mother and maternal grandparents on the left as her loving support."

Devlin's Dream – Sustainable Living. Hooked by Ginger Selman, West Newbury, Massachusetts. 52" by 59". Designed by Amy Oxford for Red Clover Rugs. Design inspired by the book, *If You're Afraid of the Dark Remember the Night Rainbow*, by Cooper Edens.
"My daughter Devlin at twenty-two is a strong woman. She introduced her parents to the field of 'sustainable living.' She believes every person does make a difference with how they live and the products they choose to buy and use in the environment. 'Devlin's Dream' depicts Devlin flying over our town with organic fields, clean rivers, and ponds that hopefully will be in our future."

Old Indian Warrior. Hooked by Carole Picard, Newburgh, New York. 45" by 30". Designed by George Kahnle for Hooked on the Creek.

Bacchanalia. Designed and hooked by Preston McAdoo, North Bennington, Vermont. 87" by 113".
"The design was taken from a black and white tile floor design I saw in a museum in Naples, Italy. I believe it came from Pompeii or Herculenium. I think it depicts a Roman fantasy of a holiday on the Nile."

Chapter 5

Accessories

Large Soft Pot. Designed and hooked by Rae Harrell, Hinesburg, Vermont. 25" by 22".
"I start by crocheting string into a form and then hooking on top of that."

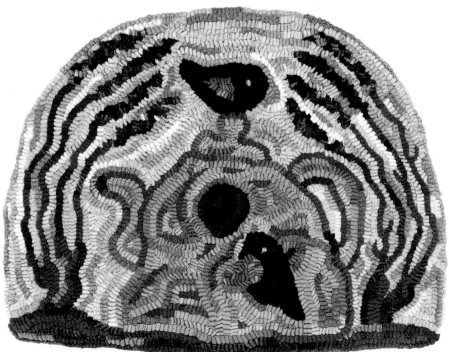

Scintiller la Reine. Designed and hooked by Jill Cooper, Riverdale, Georgia. 6" by 25".
"This crown was inspired during a class with Abby Vakay. She encouraged us all to be 'Glitter Queens.' "

Lavender Tea Cozy. Hooked by Julie Rogers, Huntington, Vermont. 16" by 12". Designed by Karen Kahle and Primitive Spirit.

Electra. (Shown front and back.) Designed and hooked by Eunice Whitney Heinlein, Avon, Connecticut. 11" by 14".

My First Handbag. (Shown front and back.) Designed and hooked by Ellen Hoffman, Cape Neddick, Maine. 16" by 15".
"The Cranberry Rug Hookers invited Phyllis Poor to demonstrate her handbag hooking. I was so inspired by Phyllis that I immediately color planned and designed my very first bag. What fun!"

Kossu Tote Bag. Hooked by Angela Foote, Barrington, New Hampshire. 18" by 22". Designed by Jane McGown Flynn.

Herati. Hooked by Nancy Z. Parcels, Mechanicsburg, Pennsylvania. 15" by 13". Designed by The House of Price, Inc.
"This pattern was my show-n-tell at Northern Teacher's Workshop for McGown Certification. The back is a recycled denim skirt. The beads, also recycled, add a bit of movement and whimsy."

Spring. Designed and hooked by Eunice Whitney Heinlein, Avon, Connecticut. 8" by 10".
"Inspired by Abby Vakay."

Purse with Orange Flower. Designed and hooked by Tracy Jamar, New York, New York. 7" by 7".
"I started making hooked purses after taking Abby Vakay's mixed media class at Shelburne in 2002."

Poinsettia Purse/Evening Bag. Designed and hooked by Jennifer Manuell, Utterson, Ontario, Canada. 8" by 7".
"Last spring, I was asked to design a pattern for the premiere issue of *A Needle Pulling Thread*, a new Canadian needle arts magazine. Wanting to appeal to hookers too, I used only novelty yarns and ribbons, with the addition of a few metallic threads to add some shine for evening."

Marianne von Werefkin. (Shown front and back.) Designed and hooked by Diane S. Learmonth, Anacortes, Washington. 13" by 13". "My rendition of Marianne von Werefkin, 1860-1938. A strong, unconventional Russian expressionist artist. Diane Phillips was my teacher."

Sheep Shoulder Bag. (Shown front and back.) Hooked by Gail Majauckas, West Newbury, Massachusetts. 11" by 10". Designed by Underhill Farm.

Trés Chick (Bag). Hooked by Suzanne Dirmaier, Waterbury Center, Vermont. 7" by 11". Design adapted by Suzanne Dirmaier from an original pattern design by M Shaw titled, "Hens on Green Door."
"I loved punching this piece, but couldn't figure out what to do with it. Frames didn't work with its dimensions. It dawned on me that I could place it on a purse. I found a great boa and suddenly it became 'Trés Chick' indeed!"

Dogwood. Hooked by Suzanne Dirmaier, Waterbury Center, Vermont. 12" by 18". Designed by Beverly Conway Designs.

"I love the whimsy and color of Bev Conway of Beverly Conway Designs. When I saw the bag she created back when the Green Mountain Rug Hooking Guild show was in Waitsfield, I knew I wanted to make one for myself. All good things come in time!"

Circles Purse. Hooked by Elizabeth M. Edwards, Williston, Vermont. 8" by 7". Designed by Beverly Conway Designs.

Floral Purse. Hooked by Elizabeth M. Edwards, Williston, Vermont. 14" by 12". Designed by Woolley Fox LLC/Barb Carroll.

83

Criss-Cross Mosaic. Designed and hooked by Celia Oliver, Shelburne, Vermont. 15" by 14".
"Mosaic tile patterns on the walls in the New York City subway stations."

Spring Pocketbook. Designed and hooked by Lesa Morrissey, Hampton, New Hampshire. 20" by 12".
"This was a Cranberry Guild workshop project. I loved making extreme textures and will probably never use it as a bag."

Purse with Blue Flowers. Designed and hooked by Tracy Jamar, New York, New York. 9" by 10".
"I started making hooked purses after taking Abby Vakay's mixed media class at Shelburne in 2002."

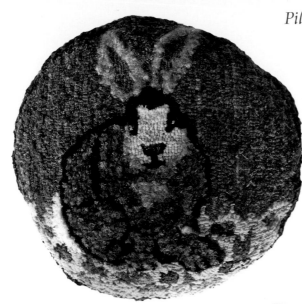

Jerry the Rabbit. Hooked by Lisa Mc-Clafferty, Wallingford, Vermont. 15" diameter. Designed by Nancy Urbanak of Beaver Brook Crafts.
"This is my first hooked piece so I picked something I would enjoy, and I love bunnies!"

Poppies and Violets Pillow. Hooked by Erika Egenes Anderson, Wesley Hills, New York. 14" diameter. Designed by Jacqueline Hansen of The 1840 House.
"I was totally fascinated with the three-dimensional effect of the Waldoboro method of hooking. Of course, working with a #3 cut is quite slow but gives a beautiful finish once hoved. I don't know which I love the most, hooking or all the wonderful people you meet along the way."

Heidi Pillow. Designed and hooked by Maya Kearn, South Londonderry, Vermont. 14" by 14".
"Our cat Heidi. We named her Heidi because she would always hide."

Black Hen With Chick Pillow. Designed and hooked by Jean Brinegar, Mt. Holly, Vermont. 16" by 13".
"Ever present amusement of chickens and chicks."

Antique Rose Pillow. Hooked by Willy Cochran, Jericho, Vermont. 14" by 15". Designed by PH Heart.
"Done in class at Shelburne Museum."

Oh My Stars! Designed and hooked by Jenny Behr, Charlotte, Vermont. 18" by 18".
"This was my first rug—inspired by my rug hooking teacher, Diane Burgess."

Brown Hen in the Sun Pillow. Designed and hooked by Jean Brinegar, Mt. Holly, Vermont. 13" by 15".
"Just the love and inspiration of chickens."

Embracing Our Love. Designed and hooked by Heather Marshall, South Burlington, Vermont. 12" by 18". "I made this rug for my boyfriend's birthday. This was my first hooking project so I wanted a design that was simple yet meaningful."

A Hippo for the Collection. Designed and hooked by Jon Ciemiewicz, Litchfield, New Hampshire. 13" by 18".
"This piece was done for my wife, to add to her collection of hippos. My son pointed out that there were no hooked hippos to go with the rest of her pieces, so I did one."

Mermaid Pillow #4. Designed and hooked by Maya Kearn, South Londonderry, Vermont. 15" by 18". "My fourth mermaid pillow. I had fun experimenting with different textures of yarn."

Mermaid Pillow. Designed and hooked by Maya Kearn, South Londonderry, Vermont. 13" by 13".
"This was inspired by the beautiful mermaid mural in the movie *Woman on Top.* This pillow was the first of five mermaid pillows I made. I gave one to each of my daughters, sewed little surprise pockets on the back, and put a gift check in each of the pockets."

"This exuberant Schnauzer of mine already saved us twice from being robbed! So small and with so much presence, she deserves to be immortalized. I had this old footstool that needed help, so why not? Here she is, forever there."

—Lucie Parrot

Fox Footstool. Designed and hooked by Nola A. Heidbreder, Saint Louis, Missouri. 5" by 13" by 8".

Celou. Designed and hooked by Lucie Parrot, Roxboro, Quebec, Canada. 19" by 12".
"This exuberant Schnauzer of mine already saved us twice from being robbed! So small and with so much presence, she deserves to be immortalized. I had this old footstool that needed help, so why not? Here she is, forever there."

Seascape Footstool. Designed and hooked by Mary I. Jameson, Brattleboro, Vermont. 12" by 16". Design inspired by "Ship Ahoy," as featured in the November/December 2004 *Rug Hooking* magazine.
"He's only two-and-a-half, but great-grandson Ben will be inheriting the footstool someday. I thought the ship was nice for a boy. The other 'grands' are girls."

Beaver Pond Footstool. Designed and hooked by Katharine Neilsen, Burlington, Vermont. 12" by 18" by 15".
"I created this pattern for a footstool as a present for my brother and his family who recently built a house on Beaver Pond in Hyde Park, Vermont."

Gremlin (Footstool). Hooked by Sandra Marquis, Wallingford, Vermont. 14" by 12" by 14". Designed by Beverly Conway and Sandra Marquis.
"This design was my idea and Beverly Conway did the drawing. Elizabeth Black helped with the colors in class. 'Gremlin' was our first family dog. He went everywhere with us and we have so many wonderful memories of him, I decided to hook him for my family."

Glad Tidings. Hooked by Angela Foote, Barrington, New Hampshire. 20" by 33". Designed by Jane McGown Flynn.

The Last Minute. Designed and hooked by Cathy Henning, Burlington, Ontario, Canada. 15" by 24".

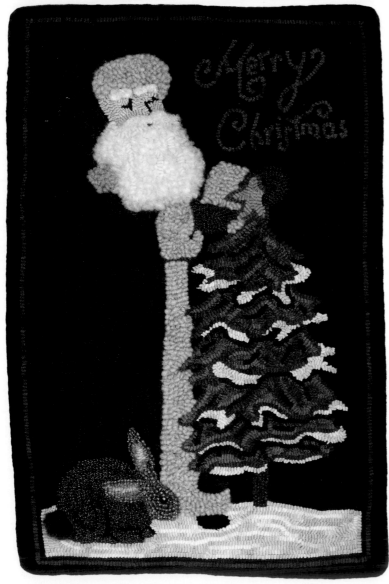

Half Moon Santa Pillow. Designed and hooked by Beverly A. King, Duxbury, Massachusetts. 18" by 13".
"I enjoy all kinds of half moon Santas. I made this pillow for a special rocking chair from my childhood. I added the hanging star for a fun and unexpected embellishment."

Left:
Victorian Santa. Hooked by Jan Tracy, Cape Elizabeth, Maine. 29" by 18". Designed by Cherylyn Brubaker, Hooked Treasures.
"This rug was hooked in class with Cherylyn. It was fun experimenting with different fibers to achieve the desired effect for Santa's beard, fur trim on his coat, and the rabbit's ears and tail."

A Tree for Ewe. Hooked by Nell Berntsen, Acworth, New Hampshire. 12" by 27". Designed by Sandra Miarecki.

"I like this design a lot and thought its simplicity would work well on a technique I wanted to try. Snipping the wool and tearing strips to be hooked worked very well on this design."

Antique Angel Rag Doll. Designed and hooked by Sunnie Andress of Old Crow Farm, Newport, Vermont. 18" by 21".

"Inspiration for this rug was an old rag doll made for me by my mother, Erma Rolph, in the 1940s! Although she is now stained and floppy, with a crooked mouth and straggly hair, I hooked her as a whimsical primitive angel."

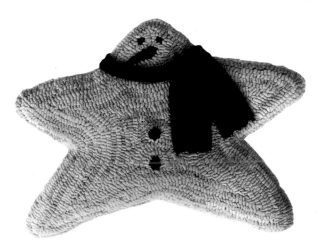

Star Snowman Pillow. Designed and hooked by Beverly A. King, Duxbury, Massachusetts. 10" by 12".

"I designed a penny style star snowman ornament and I decided I had to have it in a larger version. Therefore I designed this pillow. It is loved wherever I bring it to be shown. He is kept out on my bed all winter long."

Left:
Patriotic Snowman. Hooked by Joanna Palmer, Melrose, Massachusetts. 17" by 11". Designed by Nancy Urbanak of Beaver Brook Crafts.

Right:
Snowman. Hooked by Dorothy Panaceck, Fredericksburg, Texas. 23" by 19". Designed by Emma Lou Lais.

"Ten years ago I was in Emma Lou's workshop, working on her white pumpkin pattern. I bought this pattern and hooked it this year. It's a fun pattern to hook—very happy."

My Christmas Flower. Designed and hooked by Sue Hammond, New London, New Hampshire. 27" by 22".

Bird Stocking. Designed and hooked by Lesa Morrissey, Hampton, New Hampshire. 17" by 8".
"I enjoy making hooked holiday items."

Red Bow Wreath. Designed and hooked by Eleanor P. Hamel, Princeton, New Jersey. 22" by 41".
"I wanted a Christmas rug for in front of the fireplace. A wreath was the appropriate shape and I love drawing, coloring, and shading bows. Williamsburg fruited wreaths and garlands were the inspiration for the pears and apples. Working the greens for the wreath was a real challenge."

Midnight Stroll (2006). Designed and hooked by Jocelyn Guindon, Montreal, Quebec, Canada. 14" by 60".
"Holiday themed runner executed using a kilim technique."

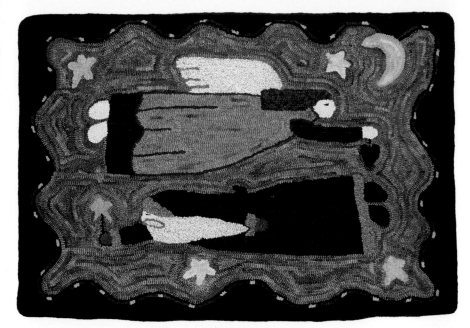

Celestial Joy. Designed and hooked by Beverly A. King, Duxbury, Massachusetts. 21" by 31". "I collect angels and love the Christmas season. I wanted to make a rug that could be displayed during the holiday season. However, my love for the rug was too great for me to pack it up with the Christmas items; I keep it out all year."

Nativity. Hooked by Mary Gebhardt, Milford, Connecticut. 20" by 25". Designed by Margo White.

Skinny Skater. Designed and hooked by Kathi Hopper, Gilford, New Hampshire. 26" by 19".
"As a teen, I spent snowy New Hampshire Sundays on my neighbor Mrs. D'arcy's pond learning to skate. Mrs. D'arcy was a character—a real 'strong woman' who coached me until I could glide over the ice. I did this rug to honor her."

Partridge in a Pear Tree. Hooked by Maureen Yates, South Burlington, Vermont. 21" by 16". Designed by Edyth C. O'Neill. "I have always loved the story of the Twelve Days of Christmas."

The Four Seasons Samplers. Designed and hooked by Toni Philbrick, Hampden, Maine. 20" by 28" each. "The same tree is shown in each season, while the other designs signify what that time of year means to me. The seasons shown here are Winter, Spring, Summer, and Autumn."

Happy Valentine's Day. Designed and hooked by Cynthia Toolin, Enfield, Connecticut. 27" by 18".

Megan's Valentine. Designed and hooked by Kathi Hopper, Gilford, New Hampshire. 19" by 17".
"My daughter Megan loves holidays, and she makes cards for our family. Valentine's Day is among her favorites. I wanted to do a 'red rug' and also capture Megan's cute face on Valentine's Day."

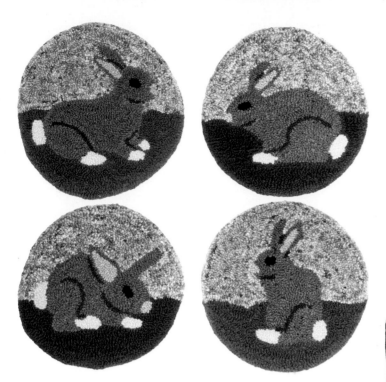

Welcome America. Designed and hooked by Eleanor de Vecchis, Cutchogue, New York. 21" by 29".

Happy Easter Chair Pads. Designed and hooked by Cynthia Toolin, Enfield, Connecticut. 15" diameter each.
"Adapted from a picture in a Dover copyright-free book. Punch needle."

Big Bird. Hooked by Deborah Walsh, Cranford, New Jersey. 43" by 31". Designed by Patsy Becker with modifications by Deborah Walsh.
"I started this rug in a class with Gail Dufresne and used some of her beautiful wool. I added the saying to turn the rug into a Thanksgiving rug."

Halloween. Hooked by Jane Ploof, Bristol, Vermont. 25" by 21". Designed by Nancy Urbanak of Beaver Brook Crafts.
"Saw this pattern and wanted a smaller project. Finished it in time for Halloween. Loved working with the oranges for the pumpkins."

Jack's Genealogy. Designed and hooked by Cynthia Toolin, Enfield, Connecticut. 33" by 50".
"This is Jack and three generations of his ancestors: his parents, grandparents, and great-grandparents. Instead of a family tree I wanted a whole genealogy."

Skinny Witch. Hooked by Janet C. Berner, South Newfane, Vermont. 23" by 8". Designed by Woolen Memories.

Glorious October. Designed and hooked by Sunnie Andress of Old Crow Farm, Newport, Vermont. 21" by 26".
"When I designed this rug, I wanted to celebrate the wonderful month of October with a touch of Halloween! The pumpkins, crows, and sunflowers were typical country images and I loved doing the border in the wild colors of Halloween costumes."

Chapter 7
Geometrics

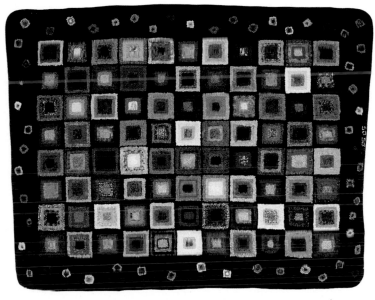

Red & Black Geometric. Designed and hooked by Carolyn Buttolph of Red House Rugs, St. Johnsbury, Vermont. 31" by 34".
"I admire the strength of design in my old, threadbare Oriental rug. Up close, its complexities are made of just a few simple elements: darks and lights, red, blue, and cream. That got me started with the geometric idea. Then I juxtaposed color, just to please myself."

Magical Squares. Designed and hooked by Peggy Stanilonis, Vergennes, Vermont. 38" by 50".
"This is my adaptation of many antique rugs. Multiple colored wools on monk's cloth. Reminiscent of using what was available to create a homey, cozy rug."

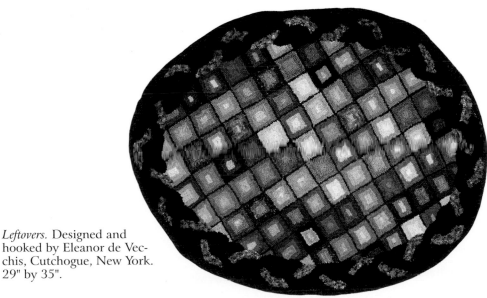

Leftovers. Designed and hooked by Eleanor de Vecchis, Cutchogue, New York. 29" by 35".

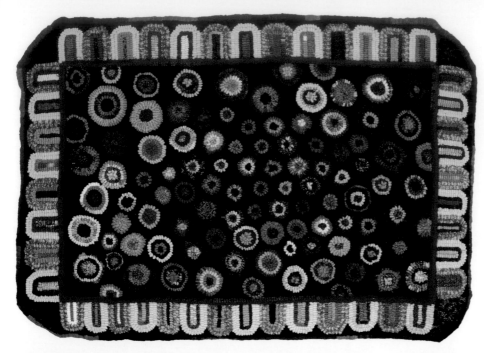

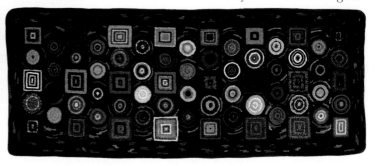

Cats' Paws, Lambs' Tongues and Dog Eared. Designed and hooked by Suzi Prather, Orlando, Florida. 21" by 30".
"My inspiration was my leftover cut wool. It was a great rug to work on in between projects."

Below:
Scrap Happy Rug. Designed and hooked by Kathy Hutchins, Cambridge, Vermont. 66" by 27".
"Imagine squash colored walls in a house that had only seen antique white and exposed beams for sixteen years. This rug was a way to tie the new colors together. Wow, what a fun way to use many colors, creating a joyful, brilliant runner for a hallway left out of the light."

Oh My Stars! Designed and hooked by Kathie Barbour, Hanover, New Hampshire. 78" by 25".
"A large antique red painted tin star was the inspiration for this rug, and I needed a runner for our hall. The title, 'Oh My Stars!' was one of my mother's favorite exclamations of surprise."

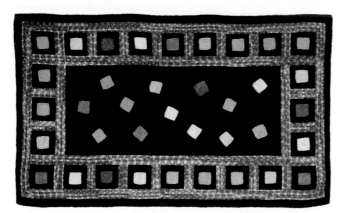

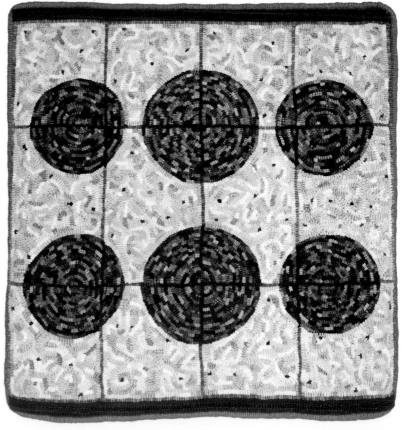

Confetti. Designed and hooked by Bev Lary, Hancock, Vermont. 32" by 54".
"Confetti ends up on the floor, so I decided to put it permanently on a rug."

Confetti Circles. Designed and hooked by Polly Alexander, Essex Junction, Vermont. 25" by 25".
"My sister wanted a small square rug with circles for her bedroom. I wanted to use an overall neutral palette, but sneak in lots of little bits of color. For the circles, I hooked no more than five loops of each color at a time. This was not a fun exercise."

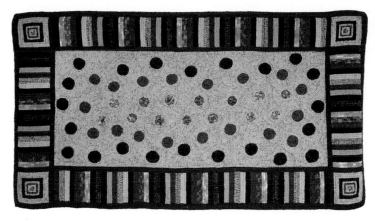

Autumn. Designed and hooked by Bev Lary, Hancock, Vermont. 32" by 57".

Grandmother's Flower Garden. Designed and hooked by Ruth McLoughlin, Rochester, Vermont. 46" by 69".
"My mother picked this quilt pattern and color scheme for a rug for her home. She passed away the following year. After many stops and starts, it's completed twelve years later in memory of her."

Parcheesi Game Board. Designed and hooked by Mary Lee O'Connor, Ballston Spa, New York. 32" by 31".
"Last year at Hooked in the Mountains I took Polly Minick's 'Let's Play,' and Iris Simpson's 'Geometric' workshops. So I decided to use one pattern to cover both topics. I found an antique Parcheesi board online and modified it to suit me."

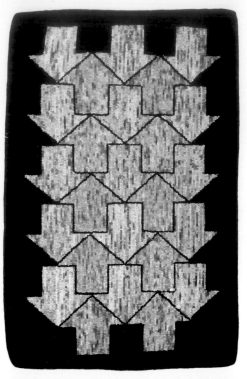

Far Left:
Patchwork Trees. Hooked by Nell Berntsen, Acworth, New Hampshire. 36" by 24". Designed by Joan Moshimer.
"When I first saw this design, I wanted to use some used green plaid wool shirts I had saved up. I had to over dye some of them to make them work."

Left:
Tessellation. Designed and hooked by Alan S. Kidder, Rochester, Vermont. 22" by 35".
"I love geometrics and patterns. My favorite colors are green and blue. Thus a repeated pattern, tessellation, popped into my mind. This was a project I have done for years with my sixth grade math classes."

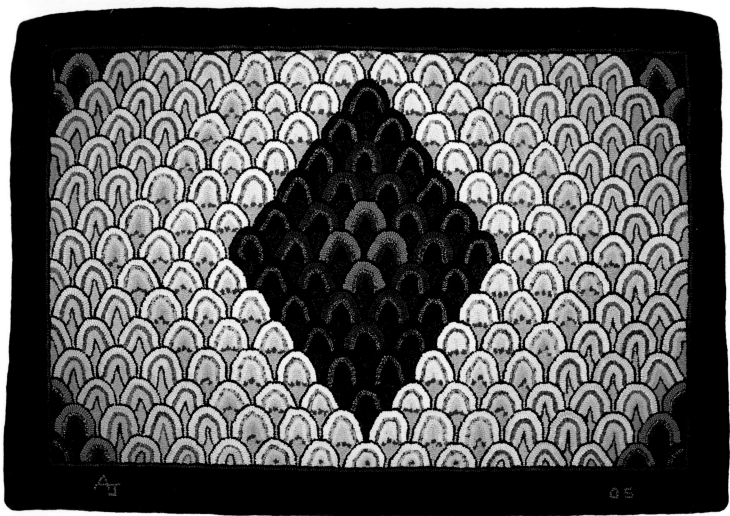

Vermont Shells. Hooked by Aurora D. Jeffrey, Calais, Vermont. 28" by 41". Designed by Jane McGown Flynn.
"I fell in love with this geometric on my first trip to the Dorr Mill Store to choose my first project. Choosing colors took two years of experimenting and rehooking many times. Each color has six values plus hounds-tooth. I love my jewel colors and am looking forward to the next geometric."

100

Scalloped Shells. Hooked by Bonnie LaPine, Essex Junction, Vermont. 32" by 64". Designed by Davey DeGraff.
"This was a Cortina Hook-In Special! Purchased at the auction, it was designed by Davey, and auctioned off with one third of it already completed and with all of the wool! What a deal."

Far Left:
JTS. Hooked by Gwenn C. Smith, Lebanon, New Hampshire. 30" by 10". Designed by Eileen McKendry and Gwenn C. Smith.
"John T. Schiffman is a person I worked for over many years. This year I will be retiring and wanted to give him something. He had admired my rugs. This design was from a note card he received from client and artist, Eileen McKendry of Rockingham, Vermont. We both admired it and I thought this was just the thing!"

Left:
GCS. Hooked by Gwenn C. Smith, Lebanon, New Hampshire. 31" by 11". Designed by Eileen McKendry and Gwenn C. Smith.
"This wall hanging is based on a watercolor by Vermont artist Eileen McKendry. The alphabet squares were interconnected by other designs that could not be adapted for inclusion in this hooking. The effect of the original design was breathtaking. Studying it, more and more was revealed."

Aztec. Designed and hooked by Bev Lary, Hancock, Vermont. 32" by 48".
"A trip to Arizona inspired the colors in this rug. A simple pattern with bright orange reminds me of desert artwork."

Log Cabin. Hooked by Susan Koehler, Hopkinton, New Hampshire. 36" by 27". Adapted by Susan Koehler from a traditional quilt design.
"This design was a great way to use up some of my stash. I wanted a 'country' feel for my guest bedroom and this is it!"

Log Cabin Geometric. Hooked by Elizabeth Morgan, Wallingford, Vermont. 38" by 32". Designed by Gail Dufresne.

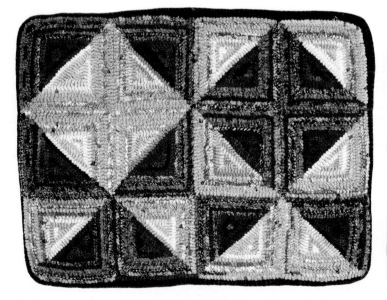

Split Geometric. Hooked by Tony Latham, Montreal, Quebec, Canada. 16" by 20". Designed by Primco Designs, The House of Price, Inc.
"A traditional quilt design. Playing with color, value, and intensity to give an old antique look. Textures add an interesting dimension."

Log Cabin. Designed and hooked by Peggie Cunningham, Hightstown, New Jersey. 40" by 33".
"I am drawn to the log cabin quilt design and a bale of leftover wool strips was my incentive."

Log Cabin. Hooked by Gail Ferdinando, Pittstown, New Jersey. 51" by 40". Designed by Gail Dufresne.
"This was hooked at a class with Gail Dufresne."

East Ironbound Squares. Hooked by Judith Dallegret, Montreal, Quebec, Canada. 32" by 52". Traditional geometric design adapted by Judith Dallegret.
"This rug was inspired by a colorful knit, square by square blanket hanging on a clothesline on East Ironbound Island in Nova Scotia. It is hooked with leftover scraps of wool."

Scrappy Geometric. Designed and hooked by Kathy Smith, Orillia, Ontario, Canada. 54" by 35".
"I love scrappy quilts. I wanted to use my leftover wool strips, so I drew a simple design on the burlap, started hooking January 9, 2006, and finished February 14, 2006."

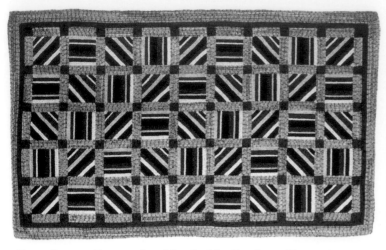

Crazy Squares. Designed and hooked by Bev Lary, Hancock, Vermont. 33" by 54".
"I was in the mood for color and a crazy pattern."

Runway Flowers. Hooked by Davey DeGraff, Hinesburg, Vermont. 18" by 54". Designed by Vermont Folk Rugs.

A Horse With No Name. Designed and hooked by Laurie M. Sybertz, Kingston, Massachusetts. 34" by 45".
"This rug was designed for my living room, combining designs I love—weathervanes and geometrics. The background was done using all the textured wool I had in the house."

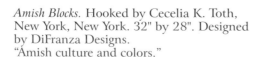

Amish Blocks. Hooked by Cecelia K. Toth, New York, New York. 32" by 28". Designed by DiFranza Designs.
"Amish culture and colors."

Square Dance. Designed and hooked by Diane Gage, Akron, Pennsylvania. 38" by 20".
"The blackbird is my favorite folk icon, and it is combined here with a familiar pattern of squares."

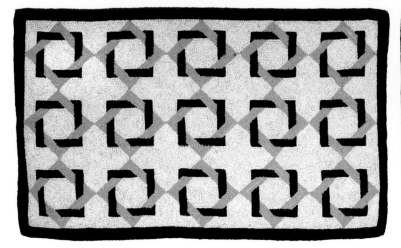

Entwined Squares. Designed and hooked by Bev Lary, Hancock, Vermont. 24" by 38".
"To use up some leftover wool, I hooked a miniature version of a quilt pattern of entwined squares."

Over-Under. Designed and hooked by Robin Garcia, Calais, Vermont. 34" by 23".
"My variation on 'hit or miss.'"

Mother's Log Cabin. Hooked by Karen Doliber, West Newbury, Massachusetts. 53" by 39". Designed by Doretta Young.
"My mother's passion in life was making log cabin quilts. I color planned this rug to match a quilt that she had made for me."

Geometric. Hooked by Ellen Hoffman, Cape Neddick, Maine. 41" by 26". Designer unknown
"Old pattern — I drew it out myself and color planned it as well. I just love the black squares. They really pull it together."

"The rug is hooked com-pletely with grocery bags... People crochet with plastic strips so I tried hooking."
—Peggy Stanilonis.

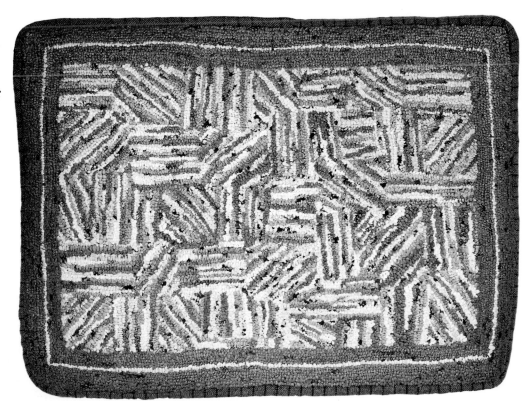

Ultimate Kitchen Rug. Designed and hooked by Peggy Stanilonis, Vergennes, Vermont. 31" by 22".
"The rug is hooked completely with grocery bags. I needed a practical rug in front of my kitchen sink. People crochet with plastic strips so I tried hooking. The strips were approximately two inches wide."

Loving Vermont. Hooked by Vicki Greene, South Londonderry, Vermont. 25" by 36". Designed adapted by Vicki Greene from a hooked rug pattern by Nola Heidbreder.
"I recently moved to Vermont and was 'adopted' by a wonderful group of hookers willing to teach me the art. This is my first rug."

Ryan and Tara's Wedding Rug. Designed and hooked by Mary Lee O'Connor, Ballston Spa, New York. 26" by 30".
"This is a wedding rug for my nephew and his fiancé. To honor their Irish heritage I choose a Celtic Knot design. My friend, Sue Charbonneau, had a knot in a circle and I made it into a heart shape. My nephew wanted plaid, thus the plaid border."

Two. Designed and hooked by Connie Baar, Tempe, Arizona. 56" by 26".
"The inspiration for the design 'Two' came from an antique rug. I wanted this rug to look old, worn, and faded. I studied the striated backgrounds of antique rugs hoping to achieve that old, naive look."

Neufs Coeurs en Cascade. Designed and hooked by Anne-Marie Littenberg, Burlington, Vermont. 21" by 20".
"A wedding gift for beloved friends Dee and Greg."

First Love. Designed and hooked by Nancy E. Baker, Shelburne, Vermont. 13" by 13".
" 'First Love' was designed in a beginner's rug hooking class taught by Diane Burgess. Diane was a fantastic teacher who encouraged me to continue with hooking. Also, these are colors I love. I plan to give this as a gift to a young couple in love."

Wild One. Designed and hooked by Carol Morris Petillo, Vinalhaven, Maine. 31" by 30".
"Number 4 of the 'Border Madness' series. I just wanted to go as wild as I could with the borders and the colors!"

Nine Stars. Designed and hooked by Eleanor de Vecchis, Cutchogue, New York. 24" by 24".

Hamadan Mat. Hooked by Sue Ryan, Lyme, New Hampshire. 39" by 26". Designed by Green Mountain Patterns.

Diamond Geometric. Designed and hooked by Nola A. Heidbreder, Saint Louis, Missouri. 22" by 28".

Autumn Glory. Designed and hooked by Carol Morris Petillo, Vinalhaven, Maine. 42" by 31".
"This is Number 6 in my 'Border Madness' series, all of which were inspired by Jule Marie Smith's workshop in 2004. Her borders were so wonderful that I decided to make a rug that was nearly all borders … and then another, and another, etc. This is the latest."

Verve II. Designed and hooked by Tricia Tague Miller, Alstead, New Hampshire. 15" diameter.
"Verve, my beloved golden retriever, was portrayed in our guild's last book, *Hooked Rugs Today.* On January 12, 2006 my boy died. In his memory, I hooked his name using folded paper to create a repeat design. For this technique (which is similar to making cut out paper snowflakes) you get a square piece of paper and fold it into a triangle. Then you write the name on it and cut out the name. (I wrote Verve.) When you unfold the triangle, you have a snowflake-like form that gives you the name and its mirror image. You can then trace this into the backing. I found the directions for this in *American Quilter Magazine, Volume XXI, Number 4.*"

Mandala One & Only. Designed and hooked by Barbara Held, Tinmouth, Vermont. 30" diameter.
"I originally designed this mandala for the table I painted for the auction at the 2005 Green Mountain Rug Hooking Guild show. I decided to hook it and as I did so, I discovered I didn't like knowing exactly where each color was going! Hence it is my mandala one and only!"

Hearts & Stars. Designed and hooked by Laurie Lausen, Minneapolis, Minnesota. 12" by 29".
"Favorite primitive motifs hooked up in my faded antique plums for a bench runner that adds a cozy warmth to our entryway. Usually piled high with mittens, it welcomes me home."

Opulence II. Designed and hooked by Emma Webber, Petaluma, California. 46" by 19".
"A friend gave me a narrow strip of burlap so I started out with a frame and a centered center and a resulting second frame—some plates outlined the circles and half-circles, and the triangles just came."

Hooked Clothesline Runner. Designed and hooked by Maddy Fraioli, Roseville, Ohio. 96" by 27".
"This clothesline rug was made using one of the historic rug techniques learned in Nola Heidbreder's class last year. Hand dyed clothesline, hand dyed rug yarn, and crochet hook. Lots of fun!"

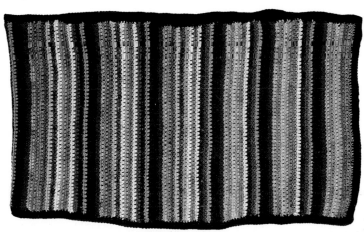

E Pluribus Unum. Hooked by Jo A. Weatherwax, Saratoga Springs, New York. 29" by 38". Designed by Marianne Fons and Liz Porter.
"I made a quilt designed by Fons and Porter and used one block to make a coordinating rug."

Stars are the Candles of the Night. Hooked by Cyndi Melendy Labelle, Hinesburg, Vermont. 24" by 32". Designed by Vermont Folk Rugs.
"I love stars! This rug was just the answer for a rug to place by my bedside."

Stars on Stripes. Hooked by Carole Picard, Newburgh, New York. 36" by 36". Designed by Polly Minick.

Isle of Shoals. Hooked by Anita Anderson, Groton, Massachusetts. 36" by 24". Designed by Karlkraft.
"I love the sea! I tried to capture the colors of the ocean, seaweed, and the granite seen along the northern New England coast. My challenge was making each of the six motifs a bit different using the same colors, unifying it with the light and darker 'granite' colors."

American Proud. Hooked by Jan Hammond, Indianapolis, Indiana. 23" by 33". Designed by George Kahnle for Hooked on the Creek.
"I hooked this rug weeks after 9/11. It explains how I felt about being an American."

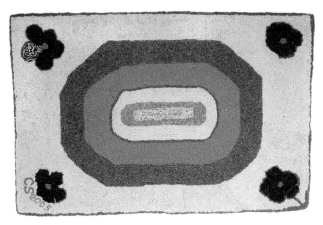

Oval Within Rectangle. Designed and hooked by Carla Straight, East Calais, Vermont. 36" by 25".

The Order of Oak Leaves. Designed and hooked by Maureen Rowe, Dollard-Des-Ormeaux, Quebec, Canada. 23" by 40".

Walking a Sacred Path. Designed and hooked by Claire O'Classen, Wallingford, Vermont. 42" diameter.
"This labyrinth from the floor of Chartes Cathedral dates from the twelfth century. The mandala form represents the journey to wholeness and reminds us to remain faithful to the process. It is a most sacred form of meditation for me. It is an archetype, a sacred path for a walking meditation, and is a spiritual tool for renewal. I am grateful to Elizabeth Morgan of Heddwch Farm for all her help and encouragement, to Diane Aines for her lettering design, and to all the Heddwch Hookers for helping me with the colors, as I am color blind."

Geometric 1910. Hooked by Kathleen Patten, Hinesburg, Vermont. 28" by 46". Designer unknown.
"This design was adapted from a pattern found in the book *American Classics – Hooked Rugs From the Barbara Johnson Collection.* The c.1910 original was done in red and blue."

Big E's Victory Lane. Designed and hooked by Andrea Sargent, Johnson, Vermont. 25" by 34".
"My boyfriend's favorite race car driver was Dale Earnhart. I designed this rug for him and gave it to him for a Christmas present."

Chapter 8

Fruit

Primitive Fruit. Hooked by Helen Johnson, Brookfield, Vermont. 20" by 40". Designed by Jane McGown Flynn.
"Just fell in love with these large fruit and had to hook them!"

Antique Pineapples. Hooked by Arlene Jackman, Vergennes, Vermont. 70" by 36". Designed by Marion Ham – Quail Hill Designs.
"All the flowers on this rug seemed overwhelming at first. But once I got started, I couldn't put it down."

Antique Pineapple. Hooked by Floreen Maroncelli, West Newbury, Massachusetts. 72" by 36". Designed by Marion Ham – Quail Hill Designs.

Antique Pineapple. Hooked by Karen Doliber, West Newbury, Massachusetts. 67" by 37". Designed by Marion Ham -- Quail Hill Designs.
"I enjoyed using numerous recycled wools in making this rug."

Antique Pineapples. Hooked by Kathy Smith, Orillia, Ontario, Canada. 69" by 38". Designed by Marion Ham – Quail Hill Designs.
"This is the rug pattern that got me interested in rug hooking. This is my third rug and I loved the challenge of picking the colors. I took a class with Jeanne Benjamin and this was my project. I love it."

#630 Espalier Pear. Hooked by Nancy Z. Parcels, Mechanicsburg, Pennsylvania. 25" by 52". Designed by Beverly Conway Designs. "The pears in this rug made for a fun place to color play. I also enjoy personalizing patterns, so I changed the bird and the tree to my liking."

Tree of Life. Hooked by Geraldine North, Hanover, New Hampshire. 23" by 30". Design adapted by Geraldine North from the Shaker's 'Tree of Life.'
"I was taken with the symmetry of the design and sense of promise in the fruit laden tree."

Apples and Pears. Hooked by Joan Mohrmann, Adirondack, New York. 24" by 46". Designed by George Kahnle for Hooked on the Creek.
"To replace a stuffed deer head over the fireplace that I have lived with for forty years."

Strawberry Basket. Hooked by Helen Johnson, Brookfield, Vermont. 26" by 42". Designed by Joan Moshimer.
"Just had to hook these great big juicy strawberries."

Summer Melon I. Hooked by Sheila M. Breton, Surry, New Hampshire. 25" by 37". Designed by Faith Williston. "This rug was hooked using natural dyes—turmeric, copper pennies, black walnuts, brazilwood, fustic, madder, and indigo."

Pineapple and Flowers. Hooked by Susan Higley, Queensbury, New York. 21" by 35". Designed by Beverly Conway Designs.

Below:
Belmont Pineapple. Hooked by Lory Doolittle, Mt. Holly, Vermont. 31" by 43". Designed by Stephanie Stouffer.
"Stephanie Stouffer and I serve on the Board of the Mt. Holly Community Historical Museum. Stephanie allowed me to hook her design to use as a raffle rug for the restoration of a historic building in Belmont, Vermont. Beverly Conway dyed the wool."

Pineapple. Hooked by Raina Mason, Charlotte, Vermont. 16" by 12". Design adapted by Raina Mason from an antique hooked rug.

Pineapple Welcome. Designed and hooked by Susan Mackey, Tinmouth, Vermont. 20" by 30".
"Designed for a class on primitive designs where one of the choices was a pineapple. I needed a new rug near my front door so this will be our welcome rug."

Cornucopia – Welcome. Hooked by Patt Weimer, Danielson, Connecticut. 23" by 26". Designed by Patt Weimer of Noah's Wife Designs.
"The person for whom this is a gift likes fall and cornucopias and her favorite color is green. This is a housewarming gift."

"And the fruits will outdo what the flowers have promised."
—Malherb, writer (1553-1628)

Welcome. Hooked by Arlene Scanlon, Essex Junction, Vermont. 12" by 9". Designed by Norma Batastini of Heart In Hand.

Pineapple. Hooked by Suzanne Jern, Wallingford, Vermont. 16" by 11". Designed by Laurice Heath, Fredericksburg Rugs.
"This is my first rug. I wanted to add it to my pineapple collection."

French Fruit. Designed and hooked by Paige Osborn Stoep, Lyons, New York. 17" by 10".
"And the fruits will outdo what the flowers have promised."
—Malherb, writer (1553-1628).

Veggie Rug. Hooked by Sarah Guiliani, South Portland, Maine. 26" by 41". Designed by Joan Moshimer.
"I love the design and the colors. I hooked it with a #3 cut."

Corn Ribbon. Designed and hooked by Cheryl Raywood, Westport, New York. 39" by 38". Design adapted by Cheryl Raywood from a Victorian bookplate design.

Fruit. Hooked by Elizabeth Morgan,
Wallingford, Vermont. 12" by 9".
Designed by Jane McGown Flynn.

Friendship Pineapple. Designed and
hooked by Shirley Zandy, Tinmouth,
Vermont. 24" by 31".

Meandering Vine With Fruit and Flowers. Designed and hooked by Celia Oliver, Shelburne,
Vermont. 8" by 47".
"This design was inspired by the wide variety of floral and fruited vines that were popular
throughout the history of art, architecture, and interior decoration."

Chapter 9

Landscapes

Victorian Scene. Designed and hooked by Janet Conner, Hiram, Maine. 32" by 52".
"I have always admired the look of old beaded bags and nineteenth century embroidery. This design was loosely inspired by two antique yarn sewn rugs from 1835, shown in Joel and Kate Kopp's book, *American Hooked and Sewn Rugs: Folk Art Underfoot.*"

"The stars are ever my guides and I never tire of singing their praises."
—Anita Landino

My Heart in the Mountain. Hooked by Linda Helms, Jeffersonville, Vermont. 45" by 37". Designed by Linda Helms and Kathy Hutchins.
"Madonna Mountain and the surrounding areas hold a special place in my heart. This rug reminds me of all of my good friends there in the F.G.C."

Winter Moon. Designed and hooked by Anita Landino, Turner, Maine. 36" by 24".
"The stars are ever my guides and I never tire of singing their praises."

Starry Night. Hooked by Liz O'Brien, South Windsor, Connecticut. 31" by 37". Designed by Vincent van Gogh with adaptations by Rae Harrell.

Below:
How the Syrup Flows. Hooked by Maureen Rowe, Dollard-Des-Ormeaux, Quebec, Canada. 24" by 38". Designed by Bluenose Patterns.
"This is a Bluenose pattern that I loved instantly. This gives me nostalgia for bygone days when horses were used in the sugar bush. It captures a moment from time past."

Winter: 4 AM Milking. Designed and hooked by Diane Kelly, Dorset, Vermont. 20" by 27".
"This rug is based on a memory from years ago when we passed a barn en route to a weekend ski trip in Vermont."

"…who among us has not felt the joy filling our hearts on a starry evening as we come down the road, over the hill, or around the bend and see before us the welcoming lights of home!"
—Sunnie Andress

Home at Last. Designed and hooked by Sunnie Andress of Old Crow Farm, Newport, Vermont. 19" by 29".
"After a day at work or a long vacation, who among us has not felt the joy filling our hearts on a starry evening as we come down the road, over the hill, or around the bend and see before us the welcoming lights of home!"

Orford. Designed and hooked by Lucie Parrot, Roxboro, Quebec, Canada. 32" by 24".
"The big pines surrounding my cottage and the view of the ski hills of Mount Orford fill me with peace and serenity. Why not place all of that on a piece to look at all the time?"

Up on Crossett Hill. Designed and hooked by Mary H. Spencer, Waterbury, Vermont. 18" by 28".
"I live in an 1860s farmhouse up on a hill in Duxbury, Vermont. This was my first big project and I thought it would help to do something I knew well. I am most proud of how my dog Millie, front and center, turned out."

Lake Champlain at Dusk. Designed and hooked by Kathleen Patten, Hinesburg, Vermont. 23" by 37".
"Inspired by my love of Lake Champlain and the Adirondacks. An experiment in hooking pines."

Love Your Neighbor. Hooked by DonnaSue Shaw, Grand Isle, Vermont. 16" by 28". Designed by Primitive Grace.
" 'Love your neighbor as yourself.' (Matt 22:59) Wouldn't it be wonderful if everyone did this? My nieces, Cierra Pepin (age eleven), and Rylee Small (age ten), helped to hook this rug."

Nat's World. Designed and hooked by Susie Stephenson, Edgecomb, Maine. 34" by 55".
"My son Nathaniel is surrounded by animals and brothers and sisters. This is his world seen through the eyes of children. Some of the creatures were drawn by his brother Joe and sister Maggie."

Bluenose #5843. Hooked by Kathy Smith, Orillia, Ontario, Canada. 29" by 59". Designed by Bluenose Patterns.
"I bought this pattern from a retired rug hooker several years before I started to rug hook. I would like to live there. Marjorie Judson helped me with this rug at a school in Ancaster, Ontario."

Irish Landscape. Hooked by Helen Wolfel, Barre, Vermont. 15" by 15". Designed by Jacqueline Hansen of The 1840 House.
"I took a three day class at the Bay View Villa with Jackye Hansen about three years ago. She showed us some creative stitches for hooking."

Ewe Too. Hooked by Jan Hammond, Indianapolis, Indiana. 23" by 30". Designed by Faith Williston and Jan Hammond.
"When I took a folk art class, I was given this pattern. When I first got it, the pattern only had the tree, rock wall, and two sheep. I was told to add things to the design so I added in everything else you see here."

Maple View Farm. Designed and hooked by Davey DeGraff, Hinesburg, Vermont. 50" by 62".
"This was my grandparents' home and the scene of happy childhood memories—the farm, the tourist cabins, and the precious time spent with family. My brother, sister, and I are all that remain, but as Ogden Nash's quote says, 'There is no end of things in the heart.' "

The Way Home. Designed and hooked by Stephanie Krauss, Green Mountain Hooked Rugs. Montpelier, Vermont. 20" by 20".
"The way home isn't always an easy journey. I began this piece years ago during a difficult time in my life and had put it aside. Only recently have I been inspired to pick it up again. Now, with a sense of joy, I completed the hooking and, so to speak, find my way home."

The Compound. Designed and hooked by Mary I. Jameson, Brattleboro, Vermont. 20" by 32".
"I call it 'The Compound' because the white house is mine and my sons live on either side. I also make quilts, so I show one on a line. I have a pocket on the back side of the rug to hold the histories of the three houses."

Autumn Sunset on the Connecticut River. Designed and hooked by Jennifer Davey, Post Mills, Vermont. 16" by 21".
"I drive along the Connecticut River almost every day and one evening the sky was beautiful and reflected into the water. It was October, hence the orange trees scattered throughout. The scene was inspirational enough to result in this effort."

Landscape. Designed and hooked by Kate Castle, Derby, Vermont. 13" by 20".
"This is a view out the back window of my new house, a landscape I enjoy every day."

Derby Pond. Designed and hooked by Kate Castle, Derby, Vermont. 11" by 13".
"The view out the back of my old house. I have sold the house since I hooked this piece and am glad to have this as a souvenir of the landscape that gave me such pleasure."

The Breaking of the Ice. Designed and hooked by Rachelle LeBlanc, Ste-Julie, Quebec, Canada. 22" by 33".
"This design was adapted from a photograph that was taken when I was seventeen, in the spring, before I left my hometown, Bouctouche, New Brunswick for college. The beauty of the spring thaw."

Otter Tracks. Designed and hooked by Jennifer Davey, Post Mills, Vermont. 16" by 25".
"I was asked to do a winter scene in a class and as I enjoy animal tracking I incorporated tracks and an otter. They are not obvious but they are there if you look carefully. The river is the Ompompanoosuc, which is in my front yard; the otter is an occasional visitor."

Summer Fields. Designed and hooked by Anne-Marie Littenberg, Burlington, Vermont. 19" by 29".
"Is there anything more calming than sunshine on a field of hay? Imagine taking a nap in the shade of the trees."

Dave and My Shadow. Designed and hooked by Martha V. North, Garrison, New York. 44" by 52".
"I made this rug from two photographs that I took as a storm was approaching, standing on top of a hill in a field on Saunder's farm."

Oriental Bench. Hooked by Barbara Pond, South Burlington, Vermont. 12" by 34". Designed by Jane McGown Flynn.
"Jenny Kuhlman asked me to assist her with the rug. She died before I had a chance to help her. She did a little work on it so I finished it for her family."

Lake in the Mountains. Hooked by Rachel Jacobs, Montpelier, Vermont. 23" by 32". Designed by Joan Moshimer.
"This landscape pattern reminds me of a lake in Vermont."

Kootenay Birches. Designed and hooked by Sara Judith, Nelson, British Columbia, Canada. 20" by 16".
"This is the view looking out my living room window east over Kootenay Lake to the Selkirk Mountains. I love the beautiful range of colors as the mountains fade into the distance."

New England Perspective. Designed and hooked by Liz O'Brien, South Windsor, Connecticut. 33" by 30".
"This is every little village you see driving through New England. The birch trees remind me of a stand of trees found in a field in front of my husband's parents' home. When designing this rug, my main focus was to achieve a strong sense of perspective. I took care to draw the village in perspective. By making the birch trees overlap the border the trees appear closer to the viewer."

Fall Birches. Designed and hooked by Eugenie Delaney, North Ferrisburgh, Vermont. 20" by 15".
"This piece was a gift for friends who live in a log cabin by a pond. When the photos they provided for inspiration didn't seem right for a rug, I decided to 'make up' what I thought it should look like out their cabin window in the fall. I wanted to juxtapose the static shapes of tree trunks and mountains with a riot of impressionistic color."

Winter is Past. Designed and hooked by Fran Irvine, Concord, New Hampshire. 23" by 28".
"This is my house, which was built in 1747 by Nathaniel and Phoebe Eastman. The beehive and bear are real. The sheep are my husband's fantasy!"

Upper Pleasant Valley. Designed and hooked by Sara Burghoff, Underhill, Vermont. 20" by 27".
"I took a photo of a barn in Cambridge, Vermont, dyed yarn, and hooked this in just two weeks to meet a deadline for a local art gallery's barn tour. I have given this rug to my oldest son for his twenty-first birthday, since he requested a Vermont scene."

Tasha Tudor's House. Designed and hooked by Marcia Kent, Wilmington, Massachusetts. 33" by 24".
"I have always admired Tasha Tudor and her passion for gardening and a simpler, more natural way of life. This rug is a tribute to her."

Island Life. Designed and hooked by Sunny Runnells, Lantzville, British Columbia, Canada. 40" by 26".
"In 1972, we moved from California to Vancouver Island with our cat, two dogs, seventeen houseplants, and VW bug. We promised to stay for a year, but time slipped away, our hair turned gray, and we're here to stay!"

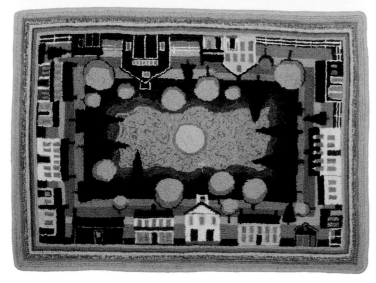

Town and Country. Designed and hooked by Barbara McKenna, Rutland, Vermont. 24" by 32".
"I lived in a Greek Revival house for twenty-three years and have loved old houses for years. I love the old buildings still standing in Vermont—the houses, barns, and outbuildings—and wanted my first rug to pay homage to them and the people who lived in them and cared for them.

On the Way to Cornwall. Designed and hooked by Sherry Kelley, Rutland, Vermont. 27" by 42".
"While I was traveling up Route 30 for a farewell visit with our friend Nancy Urbanak prior to her move to Florida, this woman wearing royal blue Wellingtons crossed the road ahead of me. With laundry blowing and the hills in the distance, this was a memory I just had to put in a rug!"

Mon Vert Cent. Designed and hooked by Mary Guay, Grand Isle, Vermont. 29" by 44".
"This is my favorite view, from the sofa in my Grand Isle living room in the fall, with my two dogs watching my husband mow the lawn, and the deer and wild turkeys grazing. Mon Vert Cent is the name of our property."

Little Bo Peep. Hooked by Diane Moore, Morgan, Vermont. 36" by 50". Designed by Heirloom Rugs.
"Pictorials are very expressive and this one reminded me of my life. This pattern is a good way to use wool to show depth and distance."

127

Claire's Gift. Hooked by Rebecca L. Cridler, Charles Town, West Virginia. 26" by 31". Designed by Rajka Kupesie.
"From the book, *Claire's Gift.* A wonderful story, sharing the gift and spirit of rug hooking for healing and growing."

The Things I love Most in the World. Designed and hooked by Maureen Rowe, Dollard-Des-Ormeaux, Quebec, Canada. 21" by 30".
"This was my first design, so I chose the things I love most in the world."

Penny Prayer Rug. Designed and hooked by Maddy Fraioli, Roseville, Ohio. 26" by 43".
"Fourth in a series of 'Prayer Rugs' inspired by Shaker prayer. 'The Pink House' is my kids' childhood home, and the sentiment expressed a foundation for their relationships with each other, and for their communities."

A Torquay Cottage. Designed and hooked by Marcy Harding, Jonesville, Vermont. 15" diameter.
"Inspired by a pattern on English Torquay pottery, this cottage came together when Jen Lavoie gave me some green wool that worked perfectly for the grass."

Torquay Scandy. Designed and hooked by Marcy Harding, Jonesville, Vermont. 15" diameter.
"Inspired by a pattern on English Torquay pottery I've collected for years. This is my first hooked piece, begun at the Green Mountain Rug School last June. Thanks to Nancy Phillips for getting me hooked, and to Stephanie Krauss and Pam Bartlett for their help with the perfect wool."

Stylized Pomegranate Tree With Quail. Designed and hooked by Janice Lacey, West Lebanon, New Hampshire. 40" by 20"
"The design is a collaborative effort with my daughter-in-law, for whom I made the rug. I showed her some general ideas and it was she who chose a pomegranate tree. I just included the quail and bird for added interest."

Heartland Sampler. Hooked by Nola A. Heidbreder, Saint Louis, Missouri. 24" by 40". Designed by Cactus Needle.
"I was inspired when I saw some redwork quilts."

Vermont Patchwork. Hooked by Davey DeGraff, Hinesburg, Vermont. 24" by 36". Designed by Vermont Folk Rugs.

Village Runner. Hooked by Karen Doliber, West Newbury, Massachusetts. 69" by 17". Designed by Barbara Brown, Port Primitives.
"I enjoyed using various textured wools in creating this runner. I have always wanted to live in a green house, thus the abundance of green houses in the village."

The Hall House. Hooked by Gwen Kjelleren, South Hero, Vermont. 25" by 69". Designed by Joan Moshimer with significant adaptations by Gwen Kjelleren.
"This rug was modified from a pattern by Joan Moshimer called '1815 House.' I adapted the original pattern to include my house, my family, our dog, and a wooden mermaid weathervane that my husband made. This rug is very special to me and will be a treasure for years to come."

Barnyard Pictorial. Hooked by Toni Philbrick, Hampden, Maine. 18" by 53". Designed by Searsport Rug Hooking.
"I started this wall hanging in a workshop, learning the special effects of prodding, pixilating, sculpting, and using roving. It was a fun piece to do, adding my own touches throughout."

Main Street - Williamstown, Massachusetts. Designed and hooked by Suzanne P. Wilkins, Williamstown, Massachusetts. 24" by 84".
"I like to do landscapes and buildings. We have a nice view of the mountains."

Snug Harbor Farm. Hooked by Anita Anderson, Groton, Massachusetts. 26" by 48". Designed by Barbara Brown, Port Primitives.

"Snug Harbor Farm is a wonderful nursery that my daughter and I visited twice on our girls' week at the beach. I had great fun hooking this rug, a birthday gift from my Mom, a reminder of hooking on the porch, walking the beaches, and mother-daughter connections."

Christopher and Ashley Looking East Over Our Field Designed and hooked by Mary Pringle, South Hero, Vermont. 13" by 21".

"This is from a photo of the grandchildren looking out toward the lake, the mountains, and the heifers. It was started in a class at Hooked in the Mountains 2005 with Michele Micarelli."

Tucson Desert. Designed and hooked by Alan S. Kidder, Rochester, Vermont. 22" by 32".

"Since my initial introduction to the Sonoran Desert in 1961 as a student at the University of Arizona, the sensory impressions have never left me. The purple mountains, various cacti, and beautiful sunsets had to be captured in a rug. The rug came to fruition in 2005."

Blue Moo. Designed and hooked by Diane Gage, Akron, Pennsylvania. 10" by 25".

"My neighbor's farm buildings and cows provided the inspiration for this rug and I used my favorite flower in the foreground."

131

Dales. Designed and hooked by Molly W. Dye, Jacksonville, Vermont. 38" by 32".
"The Dales is an area north of York, England, full of hills and dales and generally occupied by sheep and a few Vermont-like cows. A popular hiking region with sparse settlements of stone and stucco houses, void of humans and adornments."

Last Leaves. Designed and hooked by Alan S. Kidder, Rochester, Vermont. 53" by 30".
"I wanted to show originality, incorporate cut sizes, and add hoving in rocks and leaves. I was inspired by an artist from Tucson, Arizona named D. Madaras, who painted the desert in bold shapes and colors. I also wanted to hook a reflection."

Red Wings. Designed and hooked by Pandy Goodbody, Williamstown, Massachusetts. 30" by 60".
" 'These are just some of my favorite things.' Summer in northern New York on Chaumont Bay boasts an abundance of red-winged blackbirds and indescribable sunsets and sunrises. An old limestone farmhouse with its cathedral-like barn fits perfectly into the Point Salubrious landscape."

132

My Old Maple Tree. Designed and hooked by Martha V. North, Garrison, New York. 34" by 51".

NASCAR Star. Designed and hooked by Carolyn Barney, Canaan, New Hampshire. 23" by 27".
"The NASCAR theme was selected by my son Doug's children, Lauren, David and Nick. Joanne Miller gave me the checked wool for the border. She received it years ago from my sister-in-law. It was wool left from my mother-in-law's braiding days. A true family effort!"

Beauty Buick. Designed and hooked by Laura W. Pierce, Petaluma, California. 21" by 15".
"Our guild agreed to a rug challenge to match the theme of our Sonoma County Fair, which was, 'Wow, What a Ride.' My mother's car in Terrace, British Columbia, Canada brings many happy memories to me of our life in the 1950s. My dad's sawmill, the Skeena River and Sleeping Beauty complete the background."

Grover. Designed and hooked by Sherry Lowe, South Glastonbury, Connecticut. 29" by 45".
"What else would a blue Rover be called but Grover? My son, Ryan, started restoring this 1973 Series III Land Rover eleven years ago at age fifteen. It was a ground-up restoration and is his pride and joy. Grover is driven frequently and loves mud and serious off-roading."

Clipper Ship. Hooked by Brenda Williams, Valatie, New York. 29" by 43". Designed by Braid-Aid.

Sunrise on Harbour Point (2005). Designed and hooked by Jocelyn Guindon, Montreal, Quebec, Canada. 34" by 43".
"This pink house is one of the landmarks of the village of Gabarus, Nova Scotia, where I spend my summers with my family. I used a basket weave technique to give life to the shingles on the house."

Grand Old Flag. Hooked by Kathie Barbour, Hanover, New Hampshire. 30" by 31". Designed by Pris Buttler Rug Designs.

Lake House Reflections. Designed and hooked by Burma Cassidy, Rochester, Vermont. 11" by 20".
"While kayaking I see many water reflections. This is my dream house on the lake!"

The Oliver Cromwell. Hooked by Brenda Williams, Valatie, New York. 35" by 47". Designed by Edyth C. O'Neill

Three Mermaids. Designed and hooked by Susie Stephenson, Edgecomb, Maine. 30" by 26".
"Two mermaids are frolicking in the water while one rests pensively on the rocks, watching them. The background is painted and repainted. The mermaids are decorated with beads and the blond one actually has my hair."

Shipwreck and Mermaids. Designed and hooked by Susie Stephenson, Edgecomb, Maine. 16" by 18".
"Three mermaids wait for a wrecked ship to sink. The mermaids are hooked with pantyhose. The background is painted and then decorated with beads."

A Peek at Peggy's Cove. Hooked by Priscilla Buzzell, Newport, Vermont. 20" by 12". Designed by Jeanne Field.
"In August 2005, I attended the A.T.H.A. (Association of Traditional Hooking Artists) Biennial in Halifax, Nova Scotia and took the class 'A Peek at Peggy's Cove' taught by Jeanne Field. It was a great class and I enjoyed finishing our project."

Three Nights at Duncan's. Hooked by Jennifer Manuell, Utterson, Ontario, Canada. 24" by 13". Designed by Deanne Fitzpatrick. "While at Deanne Fitzpatrick's coastal landscape workshop last fall, I ate at the same local pub every night (hence the title). Deanne definitely helped me get over my obsession with 'perfect' wool—she provided all the materials: slub yarns, roving, mohair locks, unspun fleece, knits, and recycled wools."

Yoke Pond Fly Fisherman. Hooked by Karen Doliber, West Newbury, Massachusetts. 25" by 39". Designed by John Doliber.
"My husband designed this rug to depict his favorite memories of a remote fishing camp in Maine."

Montauk Lighthouse. Designed and hooked by Sarah McNamara, Greenport, New York. 18" by 17". "Every August, The Montauk Lighthouse hosts 'Lighthouse Days,' a celebration featuring a rowdy band of pirates and crafts done by sailors—including, of course, rug hooking. I've participated in this fun weekend for several years, so I hooked this view of the lighthouse as a gift to the Montauk Lighthouse Museum."

"Lighthouses represent a safe journey home. They are inspiring to artists everywhere."
—Stephanie Gibson

Lighthouse. Designed and hooked by Stephanie Gibson, St. Clairsville, Ohio. 25" by 35". "Lighthouses represent a safe journey home. They are inspiring to artists everywhere."

Chapter 10

Cabbage Roses

In April 2005, Karen Kahle from the rug company Primitive Spirit, in Oregon, came to Shelburne to teach an evening workshop at "Hooked in the Mountains" rug school. Students all worked on the same kit designed by Karen called "Cabbage Rose." Many of the finished pieces were entered in our rug show. When putting them in the book, I had to study them carefully to make sure they didn't get mixed up. Here is a challenge for you: can you match this "Cabbage Rose" with one of the other "Cabbage Roses" featured in this chapter? Answer found on page 158.

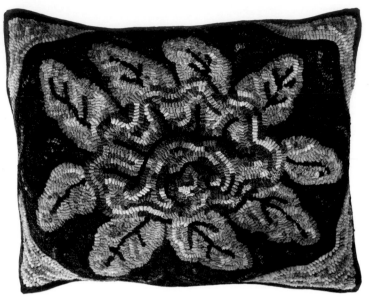

Cabbage Rose. Hooked by Priscilla Heininger, Shelburne, Vermont. 16" by 20". Designed by Karen Kahle and Primitive Spirit.
"This 'Cabbage Rose' pillow cover was started in an evening workshop taught by Karen Kahle. I modified some of the original colors to fit my own color preferences."

Cabbage Rose Pillow. Hooked by Mary Hulette, South Burlington, Vermont. 17" by 21". Designed by Karen Kahle and Primitive Spirit.
"I started hooking this at a class with Karen Kahle at last year's rug show. My friend Caryn Long of Window Works in Burlington finished it into a pillow. It looks great on our living room sofa."

Cabbage Rose. Hooked by Gwen Kjelleren, South Hero, Vermont. 16" by 20". Designed by Karen Kahle and Primitive Spirit.
"This was from a Karen Kahle kit. I made very slight color modifications, specifically withheld the blue to match a room in my house, added slightly deeper rose to the flower, and snuck in a little mustard (my favorite color)."

Cabbage Rose Pillow. Hooked by Julie Rogers, Huntington, Vermont. 16" by 20". Designed by Karen Kahle and Primitive Spirit.

Cabbage Rose Pillow. Hooked by Gail Duclos Lapierre, Shelburne, Vermont. 16" by 21". Designed by Karen Kahle and Primitive Spirit.
"From an evening workshop at Shelburne with Karen Kahle. Edge is crocheted in a scalloped design."

Cabbage Rose – Dark. Hooked by Cyndi Melendy Labelle, Hinesburg, Vermont. 16" by 20". Designed by Karen Kahle and Primitive Spirit.
"I hooked this from a kit I got last year at the evening class given by Karen Kahle."

Cabbage Rose. Hooked by Diane Burgess, Hinesburg, Vermont. 16" by 20". Designed by Karen Kahle and Primitive Spirit.
"I am a fan of Karen Kahle's designs. This pillow was finished after taking Karen's mini-workshop held during the 2005 rug show at Shelburne Museum."

The Rose. Hooked by Bonnie LaPine, Essex Junction, Vermont. 15" by 21". Designed by Karen Kahle and Primitive Spirit. "This was a kit from a mini-class Karen Kahle gave at the Green Mountain Rug Hooking Guild's Show in 2005. It was a fun class!"

Cabbage Rose Pillow. Hooked by Maureen Yates, South Burlington, Vermont. 17" by 21". Designed by Karen Kahle and Primitive Spirit. "I started this rug at a class with Karen Kahle at last year's show, I tweaked the colors a bit and may not give it to my sister like I planned."

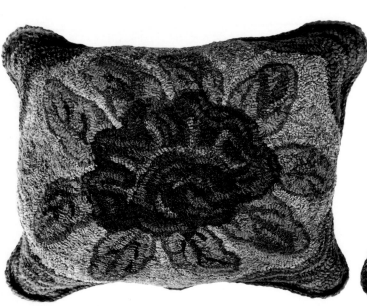

Cabbage Rose Pillow. Hooked by Fiona Cooper Fenwick, Hinesburg, Vermont. 17" by 21". Designed by Karen Kahle and Primitive Spirit.

Cabbage Rose. Hooked by Nancy Bachand, Vergennes, Vermont. 16" by 20". Designed by Karen Kahle and Primitive Spirit.

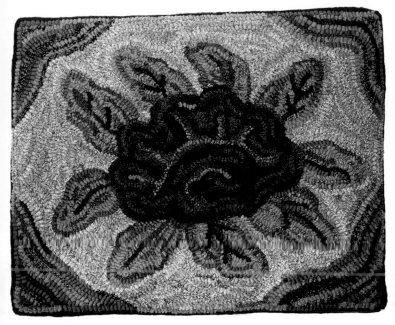

Antique Rose. Hooked by Tony Latham, Montreal, Quebec, Canada. 16" by 20". Designed by Karen Kahle and Primitive Spirit. "Limited design for blendable color workshop, Hooked in the Mountains, 2005. A challenge to use someone else's palette. Textures really give this piece an aged quality."

Cabbage Rose. Hooked by Melissa VanMarter-Rexford, Grand Isle, Vermont. 16" by 20". Designed by Karen Kahle and Primitive Spirit.
"This piece is the result of a class I took from Karen Kahle at last year's show. It was challenging to hook, forcing me to use color and contrast in new ways. It sits perfectly on a bench at home. Thank you to my friend DonnaSue Shaw for the whipping and finishing!"

Cabbage Rose. Hooked by Karen Quigley, Vergennes, Vermont. 16" by 20". Designed by Karen Kahle and Primitive Spirit. "This rug was started in a workshop at Shelburne in 2005, taught by Karen Kahle of Primitive Spirit."

Cabbage Rose. Hooked by Shirley Fortier, Williston, Vermont. 16" by 20". Designed by Karen Kahle and Primitive Spirit.

Chapter 11
Flower Baskets

We Love You. Hooked by Janice Peyton, Excello, Missouri. 24" by 29". Designed by Jo Ann and Caleb Peyton.
"A construction paper basket and flowers (true to size and color) were a very happy birthday surprise from my daughter and grandson, Jo Ann and Caleb. This rug is my gift to Jo Ann for her 40th birthday!"

"Just as the pot of hope grows one stitch at a time, and flowers grow an invisible amount each day, so our lives grow incrementally stronger with each positive thought."

—*Barbara Rosenthal*

Pot of Hope. Hooked by Barbara Rosenthal, Essex Junction, Vermont. 19" by 19". Designed by Nancy Urbanak of Beaver Brook Crafts.
"Just as the pot of hope grows one stitch at a time, and flowers grow an invisible amount each day, so our lives grow incrementally stronger with each positive thought."

September Equinox. Designed and hooked by Sue Lawler, Dorset, Vermont. 22" by 33".
"A stencil of a fruit basket in the Stencil House at Shelburne Museum, plus a book on fraktur drawings begat this rug. The colors in the rug, I felt, were appropriately bittersweet for a September equinox."

The Rose. Hooked by Loretta S. Bucceri, Danby, Vermont. 36" by 26". Designed by Mary Breed (1770).
"At our school library book sale, I found a book of embroidery. In it were many old works. I liked the one entitled, 'The Rose,' worked by Mary Breed in 1770. I made a few modifications. I think Mary would be pleased."

Basket of Joy. Hooked by Jane Griswold, Rutland, Vermont. 20" by 20". Designed by Nancy Urbanak of Beaver Brook Crafts.

Basket of Flowers. Hooked by Karen Detrick, New Lexington, Ohio. 33" by 46". Designed by Melody Hoops, Fleecewood Farms Designs.
"The background color came first, followed by a birthday card, and Melody Hoops drew this wonderful pattern just for me."

Bird in the Flowers. Designed and hooked by Gwendolyn S. Gallup, St. Albans, Vermont. 27" by 25".
"I designed 'Bird in the Flowers' originally as a penny rug. After its completion, I decided to hook the pattern as well."

Quilt Square Sampler. Hooked by Sandi Goldring, Essex Junction, Vermont. 39" by 39". Designer unknown.

Blue Basket Antique. Hooked by Jean Brana, South Burlington, Vermont. 36" by 52". Designed by Edyth C. O'Neill.

Love Birds. Hooked by Melonie Bushey, Vergennes, Vermont. 28" by 35". Designed by Eugenie Delaney for Beverly Conway Designs.

Wicker Basket. Hooked by Jane Ploof, Bristol, Vermont. 20" by 18". Design adapted from the folk art of M Shaw by Kris Miller and Spruce Ridge Studios.
"Loved this pattern and wanted to branch out a little with the basket."

Schwenkfelder Flower Basket. Hooked by Karl Gimber, Carversville, Pennsylvania. 21" by 21". Design adapted from a fraktur by Mary Jo Gimber.
"The inspiration for this design is from a fraktur bookplate in the Schwenkfelder Library. In September 2006, the rug was raffled to benefit the Schwenkfelder Library and Heritage Center, and Hunterdon County Rug Artisans Guild."

Flower Basket. Hooked by Rebecca L. Cridler, Charles Town, West Virginia. 26" by 20". Designed by Jane McGown Flynn.
"I had to spend some time indoors. This was fun to work on."

145

Three Red Posies. Designed and hooked by Leslie Goldring, Ferrisburg, Vermont. 34" by 44".
"In paintings, it's always a vase of flowers; in rugs, it's usually a bowl. After noticing this trend I just had to join it."

Sue's Flower Basket. Designed and hooked by Susan DeGregorio, Salem, New Hampshire. 25" by 29".

Posy Pot and Chicks. Hooked by Willy Cochran, Jericho, Vermont. 25" by 36". Designed by Lib Callaway.

Basket of Flowers. Hooked by Linda L. Smith, Fair Haven, Vermont. 25" by 40". Design adapted from an antique rug. "This rug was adapted from an 1880 rug. I added the side ribbons and bow from a counted cross-stitch pattern. The blue color in the original was bright so I used turquoise instead. I hope I have honored the original rug hooker by recreating this wonderful rug."

Spring. Hooked by Lynn Soule, North Hero, Vermont. 20" by 33". Designed by Green Mountain Patterns. "Love the primitive look of this rug!"

Flower Pot Primitive. Hooked by Robyn Hodges, Topsfield, Massachusetts. 24" by 55". Design adapted from the folk art of M Shaw by Kris Miller and Spruce Ridge Studios. "I loved this design by M Shaw. I changed the flowers to match my front hall and just had fun hooking with a #9 cut for the first time."

KD's Promise. Hooked by Janet Myette, Glens Falls, New York. 31" by 65". Designer unknown. "My second rug."

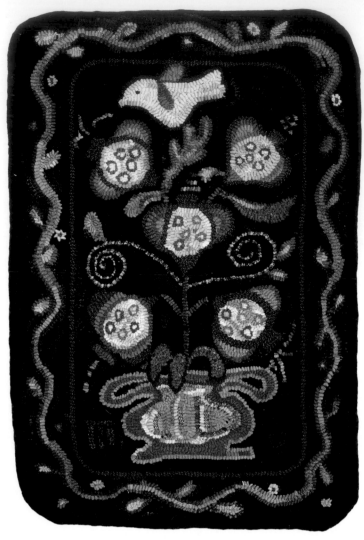

Five Pomegranates. Hooked by Ivi Nelson Collier, Nottingham, Maryland. 28" by 20". Designed by Susan Feller, Ruckman Mill Farm.

Pomegranates. Hooked by Suzanne Kowalski, South Burlington, Vermont. 30" by 18". Designed by Susan Feller, Ruckman Mill Farm.
"As soon as I saw this rug, I visualized it in colors I love. This was fast and fun."

Compote With Camellias. Hooked by Julie Rogers, Huntington, Vermont. 24" by 38". Designed by Karen Kahle and Primitive Spirit.

Border Series #5 – Flower Basket. Designed and hooked by Judy Quintman, Wilmington, North Carolina. 29" by 38".
"I wanted to incorporate the circles, triangles, and cats' tongues, then I had to find a center design. I wanted to repeat the shapes and my flower basket developed."

Flowers in Red. Designed and hooked by Gwendolyn S. Gallup, St. Albans, Vermont. 31" by 48".
"I chose the hand dyed wools first before designing this rug. I wanted to showcase the heavily mottled red in large flowers. The diamond border seemed perfect to complement the floral design."

Bird in Flowers. Hooked by Lynn Soule, North Hero, Vermont. 25" by 28". Designed by Gwendolyn S. Gallup.
"This is my first rug! I took a class in June 2005 and completed this in November 2005. I was completely hooked. It is the most relaxing hobby I've ever done."

Hooked on Rugs. Hooked by Ivi Nelson Collier, Nottingham, Maryland. 24" by 20". Designed by Gary Head and Cindy Andrews.
"This rug was featured in the January/February 2006 edition of *Rug Hooking* magazine in an article by Nancy Parcels."

Bernie's Pot. Hooked by Kathleen Patten, Hinesburg, Vermont. 26" by 38". Designer unknown.
"This was bought as an unsigned antique burlap pattern and was inspired by Karen Kahle's dye books."

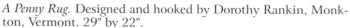

A Penny Rug. Designed and hooked by Dorothy Rankin, Monkton, Vermont. 29" by 22".
"This rug was inspired by a friend's early penny rug. The charm and naivety of these rugs has always appealed to me. This is a hooked penny rug!"

Below:
Primitive Poppies. Designed and hooked by Nancy W. Urbanak, Titusville, Florida. 25" by 46". Design adapted from the folk art of M Shaw by Kris Miller and Spruce Ridge Studios.
"For me, rugs are like music. I associate phases of my life with when a particular rug was being hooked, or certain music was popular. This is my healing rug. Its creation spans the year and a half it took for me to feel whole again after a twenty-eight year marriage and unpleasant divorce."

Chapter 12

Rug Hooking at the Youville Centre

The theme of this year's rug show was "Strong Women." With this in mind, there are some remarkably strong young women from Canada's capital city of Ottawa, Ontario, who have been working enthusiastically on their own rugs. Their work was not in our show, but their story is so inspiring that I wanted to share it with you. The rug hookers are teenage mothers from the ages of fifteen to twenty-one who are completing high school while raising their babies and small children. They also have jobs in their community and are working towards successful careers. Once a week they meet to work on their hooked rugs, using the punch needle method. Their teacher, Ainslie Kuryliw, creator of the rug hooking program, tells us more:

"The M. F. McHugh Education Centre is a unique high school educational facility, known as the Youville Centre. The school supports the continuing education of forty-eight teenage mothers who wish to further their education after an interruption of studies as a result of the birth of a child. The students who have submitted rugs have all been part of the cooperative education program at McHugh during the 2005-2006 school year."

"Over time, as we discussed the intricacies of the world of work, parenting responsibilities, academics, personal relationships, and life in general, we saw the rugs taking shape. Throughout the entire process, the young mothers rallied around one another, offering words of encouragement, from the designing process and color scheme, use of a light table and staple gun, and proper punch needle technique, to managing a needle and thread. Every part of this project involved team building and problem solving, which resulted in remarkable camaraderie in class. Students found relaxation in the smoothness of the wood handle and the rhythm of the punch needle."

"During school rug hooking sessions, my students and I often spoke about our good fortune in having met Amy Oxford through my contact with Jessica Thomas, a talented rug designer from Ottawa, Canada. (While taking a rug hooking class offered by Jessica, I was inspired by her enthusiasm and decided to teach the punch needle technique to my own students.) At Jessica's suggestion, I contacted Amy and she helped me develop a plan … now we find ourselves published in her latest book! My students and I recognize and value the strength of this long-distance friendship built on a mutual love of punch needle rug hooking."

Two of the rug hookers are not featured here, not because their rugs weren't wonderful, but because they depicted popular characters that we cannot include for copyright reasons. Congratulations to Robin Mathews, age 21, and Melissa Miron, age 18, for creating and completing these beautiful rugs.

In the correspondence I have gotten from these young mothers, I have been touched by their devotion to their babies, and impressed by their commitment to a bright future for themselves and their children. On behalf of The Green Mountain Rug Hooking Guild, I would like to wish all of the Youville Centre rug hookers our best wishes for success and happiness in the future. We are very proud of you.

Egyptian Eye. Designed and hooked by Amanda Denis, Age 19. 12" by 18".
"My nickname is 'Pink' and I incorporated that idea as I developed the color scheme for my rug. I will hang this up in the home I share with my son Darius. I have enrolled in a bartending course for fall, 2006."

My Team. Designed and hooked by Amanda McKay, Age 18. 17" by 20".
"My son Jakob and I are big hockey fans; our team is called the Ottawa Senators. I designed the rug in red, white, and black to match the team colors. 'Go Sens Go!'"

Pretty Baby. Designed and hooked by Ashley Gauthier, Age 20. 16" by 23".
"I enjoyed learning how to punch hook rugs and will pick up the leisure activity at home. My rug is for my daughter, Olivia. It is my plan to work in accounting after completing my college studies."

Sweet Dreams. Designed and hooked by Brianne Marvin, Age 18. 20" by 23".
"The reason I chose this design is because I was pregnant with my first child, Rowen Kenneth, and I wanted to make it for his room. My son has since been born. My plans are to finish high school and go into nursing."

Zack's Room. Designed and hooked by Corrie Yuill, Age 20. 18" by 22".
"I chose this design to give to my son, Zackary, a special something with his name on it. I will put it in his bedroom. After graduation in June 2006 my plans are to go into esthetics."

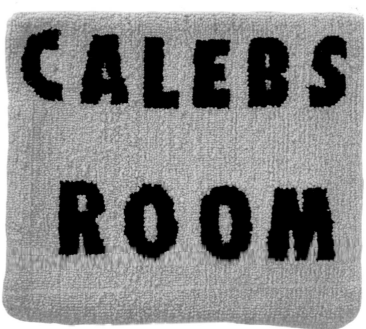

Wish. Designed and hooked by Samantha Booth, Age 19. 17" by 21".
"This rug was made for the house I share with my son Damelon. I drew the pattern freehand and was very happy with the color scheme and shading of the trees. I will graduate in June 2006 and study the art of massage therapy."

Connie. Designed and hooked by Jennifer Leeman, Age 21. 13" by 19".
"I designed this for my daughter, Connie. I chose an assortment of variegated colors as I planned out my project. I love working with fiber arts and hope to study fashion one day."

Caleb's Room. Designed and hooked by Sandra Vawer, Age 18. 19" by 21".
"I worked on this for my son, Caleb. I was happy to finish this rug for him and have other rug projects in mind. I really enjoy handicrafts and will continue to do rugs as I study nursing."

153

Vendors

On opening night of the rug show, as I was walking down the stairs into the vendors' area (located in the basement of The Round Barn), I looked down on all of the booths full of gorgeous wool. I was reminded of the fairy tale about Rumplestiltskin, who started at bedtime and somehow magically spun all of the straw into gold by morning. I began to daydream … if we rounded up all 150 rug hookers who were here at the reception and locked them in the basement—would they be able to hook all the wool into rugs by morning? My guess is that they would. No problem. I continued daydreaming and at dawn, all the wool was gone and the rug hookers were asleep on their finished rugs. Having craftily smuggled all the hor's d'oevres and sweets in with them when they were rounded up, they had a marvelous night, turning a hostage situation into a party with lots of jokes, stories, and raucous laughter. This wool may not be straw, but these people really know how to spin it into gold. Rug hookers are always being offered challenges: hook a self portrait, embellish a chicken, or hook a "strong woman." An all-night hook-in … now that would be the biggest challenge to date! I walked down a few more steps into the basement and came out of my reverie: "Okay Amy, snap out of it, now what was I actually here for? Oh yes, a #3 blade for my Rigby cutter and some spot-dyed blue wool…"

American Country Rugs
Lucille Festa
4743 Route 315
Pawlet, VT 05761
(Studio located in East Rupert)
(802) 325-2543
E-mail: Lucillefesta@hotmail.com

Beaver Brook Crafts
Nancy Urbanak
4959 Squires Drive
Titusville, FL 32796
(321) 268-2193
E-mail: NancyUrbanak@yahoo.com

Beverly Conway Designs
Beverly Conway
1859 Munger Street
Middlebury, VT 05753
(802) 388-7742
E-mail: prism@together.net

The Dorr Mill Store
Terry Dorr
PO Box 88, 22 Hale Street
Guild, NH 03754
(603) 863-1197 or (800) 846-DORR
E-mail: dorrmillstore@nhvt.net
Website: DorrMillStore.com

Fluff & Peachy Bean Designs
Nancy D. Jewett
PO Box 30, 2126 US Route 7
Pittsford, VT 05763
(802) 483-2222
E-mail: njewett@aol.com

Green Mountain Hooked Rugs, Inc.
Stephanie Krauss
2838 County Road
Montpelier, VT 05602
(802) 223-1333
E-mail: vtpansy@GreenMountain
    HookedRugs.com
Web: GreenMountainHookedRugs.com

Hooked Treasures
Cherylyn Brubaker
6 Iroquois Circle
Brunswick, ME 04011
(207) 729-1380
E-mail: tcbru@suscom-maine.net
Website: www.hookedtreasures.com

Kinderhook Bed & Breakfast
Jayne Hester
67 Broad Street
Kinderhook, NY 12106
(518) 758-1850
E-mail: Kinderhookb-b@Berk.com
Website: KinderhookBandB.com

Little Victories Rug Designs
Diane Phillips
19 Great Garland Rise
Fairport, NY 14450
(585) 223-0038
E-mail: rugsdp@rochester.rr.com

Liziana Creations
Diana and Liz O'Brien
595 Patten Hill Road, PO Box 310
Shelburne Falls, MA 01370
(413) 625-9403
E-mail, Diana: Diana@galaxy.net

Suggested Reading

Compiled by Anne-Marie Littenberg

Books

Allard, Mary. *Rug Making: Techniques and Design*. Philadelphia, Pennsylvania: Chilton Book Company, 1963.

Aller, Doris. *Handmade Rugs*. Menlo Park, California: Lane Publishing Company, c. 1953.

Batchelder, Martha. *The Art of Hooked-Rug Making*. Peoria, Illinois: The Manual Arts Press, 1947.

Beatty, Alice, and Mary Sargent. *Basic Rug Hooking*. Harrisburg, Pennsylvania: Stackpole Books, 1990.

Beatty, Alice, and Mary Sargent. *The Hook Book*. Harrisburg, Pennsylvania: Stackpole Books, 1977.

Black, Elizabeth. *Hooked on the Wild Side*. Lemoyne, Pennsylvania: Rug Hooking Magazine, 2004.

Boswell, Thom, ed. *The Rug Hook Book: Techniques, Projects and Patterns for This Easy, Traditional Craft*. New York: Sterling Publishing Co., Inc., 1992.

Bramlett, Carol, and Leslie Hoy. *A Celebration of Hand-Hooked Rugs VIII*. Edited by Patrice A. Crowley. Harrisburg, Pennsylvania: Stackpole Books, 1998.

Brown, Barbara Evans. *Preserving the Past in Primitive Rugs*. Harrisburg, Pennsylvania: Stackpole Books, 2005.

Burton, Mary Sheppard. *A Passion for the Creative Life: Textiles to Lift the Spirit*. Edited by Mary Ellen Cooper. Germantown, Maryland: Sign of the Hook Books, 2002.

A Celebration of Hand-Hooked Rugs. Harrisburg, Pennsylvania: Stackpole Books, 1991.

Carroll, Barbara. *The Secrets of Primitive Hooked Rugs: Your Complete Guide to Hooking a Primitive Rug*. Harrisburg, Pennsylvania: Stackpole Publications, 2004.

Carroll, Barbara. *Woolley Fox American Folk Art Rug Hooking*. Urbandale, Iowa: Landauer Corporation, 2005.

Cooper, Mary Ellen, ed. *A Celebration of Hand-Hooked Rugs II*. Harrisburg, Pennsylvania: Stackpole Books, 1992.

Cooper, Mary Ellen, ed. *A Celebration of Hand-Hooked Rugs III*. Harrisburg, Pennsylvania: Stackpole Books, 1993.

Cox, Verna. *Rug Hooking and Braiding Made Easy*. Atlanta, Georgia: Cox Enterprises, 2003.

Crouse, Gloria E. *Hooking Rugs: New Materials, New Techniques* (and companion video). Newtown, Connecticut: The Taunton Press, 1990.

Cross, Pat. *Purely Primitive: Hooked Rugs from Wool, Yarn, and Homespun Scraps*. Woodinville, Washington: Martingale and Company, 2003.

Cross, Pat. *Simply Primitive: Rug Hooking, Punchneedle, and Needle Felting*. Woodinville, Washington: Martingale and Company, 2006.

Crowley, Patrice A., ed. *A Celebration of Hand-Hooked Rugs V*. Harrisburg, Pennsylvania: Stackpole Books, 1995.

Crowley, Patrice A., ed. *A Celebration of Hand-Hooked Rugs VI*. Harrisburg, Pennsylvania: Stackpole Books, 1996.

Crowley, Patrice A., ed. *A Celebration of Hand-Hooked Rugs VII*. Harrisburg, Pennsylvania: Stackpole Books, 1997.

Crowley, Patrice A., ed. *A Rug Hooker's Garden*. Harrisburg, Pennsylvania: Rug Hooking Magazine, 2000.

Darr, Tara. *Wool Rug Hooking*. Iola, Wisconsin: Krause Publications, 2005.

Davies, Ann. *Rag Rugs: How to Use Ancient and Modern Rug-Making Techniques to Create Rugs, Wallhangings, Even Jewelry – 12 Projects*. New York: Henry Holt and Company, Inc., 1992.

Davis, Mildred J. *The Art of Crewel Embroidery*. New York: Crown Publishing, 1962.

Davis, Mildred J. *Early American Embroidery Designs*. New York: Crown Publishing, 1969.

Davis, Mildred J., ed. *Embroidery Designs, 1780-1820*; From the manuscript collection, The Textile Resource and Research Center, the Valentine Museum, Richmond, Virginia. New York, Crown Publishing, 1971.

Eber, Dorothy H. *Catherine Poirier's Going Home Song*. Halifax, Nova Scotia: Nimbus Publishing, 1994.

Farr, Christopher, Mathew Bourne, and Fiona Leslie. *Contemporary Rugs*. London: Merrell Publishers Limited, 2002.

Felcher, Cecelia. *The Complete Book of Rug Making: Folk Methods and Ethnic Designs*. New York: Hawthorne Books, 1975.

Field, Jeanne. *Shading Flowers: The Complete Guide for Rug Hookers*. Harrisburg, Pennsylvania: Stackpole Books, 1991.

Fitzpatrick, Deanne. *Hook Me A Story: The History and Method of Rug Hooking in Atlantic Canada*. Halifax, Nova Scotia: Nimbus Publishing, Ltd., 1999.

Halliwell, Jane E. *The Pictorial Rug: Everything You Need to Know to Hook a Realistic, Impressionistic, or Primitive Picture With Wool*. Rug Hooking Magazine's Framework Series 2000, Edition V. Lemoyne, Pennsylvania: M. David Detweiler, 2000.

Henry Ford Museum & Greenfield Village. *Edward Sands Frost's Hooked Rug Patterns*. Dearborn, Michigan: Edison Institute, 1970.

Hoy, Leslie, and Sarah Wilt. *A Celebration of Hand-Hooked Rugs IX*. Edited by Patrice A. Crowley. Harrisburg, Pennsylvania: Stackpole Books, 1999.

Hoy, Leslie. *A Celebration of Hand-Hooked Rugs X*. Edited by Patrice A. Crowley. Harrisburg, Pennsylvania: Stackpole Books, 2000.

Hoy, Leslie. *A Celebration of Hand-Hooked Rugs XI*. Edited by Patrice A. Crowley. Lemoyne, Pennsylvania: Rug Hooking Magazine, 2001.

Hoy, Leslie. *A Celebration of Hand-Hooked Rugs XII*. Edited by Wyatt R. Myers. Lemoyne, Pennsylvania: Rug Hooking Magazine, 2002.

Johnson, Barbara. *American Classics: Hooked Rugs from the Barbara Johnson Collection*. Jenkintown, Pennsylvania. Squibb Corp., 1988.

Kennedy, MacDonald, ed. *A Celebration of Hand-Hooked Rugs IV*. Harrisburg, Pennsylvania: Stackpole Books, 1994.

Kent, William W. *The Hooked Rug*. New York: Tudor Publishing Company, 1930.

Kent, William W. *Hooked Rug Design*. Springfield, Massachusetts: The Pond Ekberg Company, 1949.

Kent, William W. *Rare Hooked Rugs and Other: Both Antique & Modern*. Springfield, Massachusetts: The Pond-Ekberg Company, 1941.

Ketchum, William C., Jr. *Hooked Rugs: A Historical and Collectors Guide: How to Make Your Own*. New York: Harcourt, Brace, Jovanovich, 1976.

King, Mrs. Harry. *How To Hook Rugs*. Little Rock, Arkansas: D. P. and L. Company, 1948.

Kopp, Joel, and Kate Kopp. *American Hooked and Sewn Rugs: Folk Art Underfoot*. New York: E. P. Dutton, Inc., 1985.

Lais, Emma Lou, and Barbara Carroll. *Antique Colours for Primitive Rugs: Formulas Using Cushing Acid Dyes*. Kennebunkport, Maine: W. Cushing & Company, 1996.

Lais, Emma Lou, and Barbara Carroll. *American Primitive Hooked Rugs: Primer for Recreating Antique Rugs*. Kennebunkport, Maine: Wildwood Press, 1999.

Lawless, Dorothy. *Rug Hooking and Braiding For Pleasure and Profit*. New York: Thomas Y. Crowell, 1962.

Lincoln, Maryanne. *Recipes From the Dye Kitchen*. Harrisburg, Pennsylvania: Rug Hooking Magazine, 1999.

Lincoln, Maryanne. *Maryanne Lincoln's Comprehensive Dyeing Guide*. Lemoyne, Pennsylvania: Rug Hooking Magazine, 2005.

Linsley, Leslie. *Hooked Rugs: An American Folk Art*. New York: Clarkson N. Potter, Inc., 1992.

Logsdon, Roslyn. *People and Places: Roslyn Logsdon's Imagery In Fiber*. Rug Hooking Magazine's 1998 Framework Series Edition. Harrisburg, Pennsylvania: David Detweiler, 1998.

Lovelady, Donna. *Rug Hooking For the First Time*. New York: Sterling Chapelle, 2005.

Mather, Anne D. *Creative Rug Hooking*. New York: Sterling Publishing Company, 2000.

McGown, Pearl K. *Color in Hooked Rugs*. West Boylston, Massachusetts: Pearl K. McGown, 1954.

McGown, Pearl K. *The Lore and Lure of Hooked Rugs*. West Boylston, Massachusetts: Pearl K. McGown, 1966.

McGown, Pearl K. *Persian Patterns*. West Boylston, Massachusetts: Pearl K. McGown, 1958.

McGown, Pearl K. *You...Can Hook Rugs*. West Boylston, Massachusetts: Pearl K. McGown, 1951.

Minick, Polly and Laurie Simpson. *Everyday Folk Art: Hooked Rugs and Quilts to Make*. Woodinville, Washington: Martingale and Company, 2005.

Minick, Polly and Laurie Simpson. *Folk Art Friends: Hooked Rugs and Coordinating Quilts*. Woodinville, Washington: Martingale and Company, 2003.

Montell, Joseph. *The Art of Speed Tufting*. Santa Ana, California: RC Rug Crafters, 1976.

Moshimer, Joan. *The Complete Rug Hooker: A Guide to the Craft*. Boston, Massachusetts: New York Graphic Society, 1975.

Moshimer, Joan. *Hooked on Cats: Complete Patterns and Instructions for Rug Hookers*. Harrisburg, Pennsylvania: Stackpole Books, 1991.

Myer, Wyatt, ed., *Basic Rug Hooking*. Lemoyne, Pennsylvania: Rug Hooking Magazine, 2002.

Myers, Lori. *A Celebration of Hand-Hooked Rugs XIII: The Finest of Fiber Art*. Edited by Wyatt R. Myers. Lemoyne, Pennsylvania: Rug Hooking Magazine, 2003.

Olson, Jane. *The Rug Hooker's Bible: The Best from 20 Years of Jane Olson's Rugger's Roundtable*. Edited by Gene Shepherd. Harrisburg, Pennsylvania: Stackpole Publications 2006.

Oxford, Amy. *Hooked Rugs Today*. Atglen, Pennsylvania: Schiffer Publishing Ltd., 2004.

Oxford, Amy. *Punch Needle Rug Hooking: Techniques and Designs*. Atglen, Pennsylvania: Schiffer Publishing Ltd., 2003.

Parker, Xenia L. *Hooked Rugs & Ryas: Designing Patterns and Applying Techniques*. Chicago, Illinois: Henry Regency Company, 1973.

Peladeau, Mildred C. *Art Underfoot: The Story of the Waldoboro Hooked Rugs*. Lowell, Massachusetts: American Textile History Museum, 1999.

Peverill, Sue. *Make Your Own Rugs: A Guide to Design and Technique*. London: Hamlyn Publishing Group, Ltd., 1989.

Phillips, Anna M. *Hooked Rugs and How to Make Them*. New York: Macmillan, 1925.

Ries, Estelle H. *American Rugs*. Cleveland, Ohio: The World Publishing Company, 1950.

Rex, Stella H. *Choice Hooked Rugs*. New York: Prentice-Hall, 1953.

Rex, Stella H. *Practical Hooked Rugs*. Ashville, Maine: Cobblesmith, 1975.

Rug Hooking Magazine – the entire *Framework and Celebrations* series.

A Rug Hooking Book of Days Featuring the Fiber Art of Polly Minick. Harrisburg, Pennsylvania: Stackpole Books, 1998.

Rug Hooker's Garden: 10 Experts Teach You How to Hook a Veritable Bouquet of Blossoms. Harrisburg, Pennsylvania, Stackpole Books, 2005.

Siano, Margaret and Susan Huxley. *The Secrets of Finishing Hooked Rugs*. Lemoyne, Pennsylvania: Rug Hooking Magazine, 2003.

Stratton, Charlotte K. *Rug Hooking Made Easy*. New York: Harper and Brothers Publishers, 1955.

Taylor, Mary P. *How To Make Hooked Rugs*. Philadelphia: David McKay Company, c. 1930.

Tennant, Emma. *Rag Rugs of England and America*. London: Walker Books, 1992.

Turbayne, Jessie A. *The Big Book of Hooked Rugs: 1950s-1980s*. Atglen, Pennsylvania: Schiffer Publishing Ltd., 2004.

Turbayne, Jessie A. *Hooked Rugs: History and The Continuing Tradition*. West Chester, Pennsylvania: Schiffer Publishing Ltd., 1991.

Turbayne, Jessie A. *Hooked Rug Treasury*. Atglen, Pennsylvania: Schiffer Publishing Ltd., 1997.

Turbayne, Jessie A. *The Hooker's Art*. Atglen, Pennsylvania: Schiffer Publishing Ltd., 1993.

Turbayne, Jessie A. *The Complete Guide to Collecting Hooked Rugs: Unrolling the Secrets*. Atglen, Pennsylvania: Schiffer Publishing Ltd., 2004.

Underhill, Vera B., and Arthur J. Burks. *Creating Hooked Rugs*. New York: Coward-McCann, 1951.

Vail, Juju. Rag Rugs: *Techniques in Contemporary Craft Projects*. Edison, New Jersey: Chartwell Books, 1997.

Von Rosenstiel, Helene. *American Rugs and Carpets From the Seventeenth Century to Modern Times*. New York: Morrow, c. 1978.

Walch, Margaret, and Augustine Hope. *Living Colors: The Definitive Guide to Color Palettes Through the Ages*. San Francisco: Chronicle Books, 1995.

Waugh, Elizabeth. *Collecting Hooked Rugs*. New York, London: The Century Company, 1927.

Wilcox, Bettina. *Hooked Rugs for Fun and Profit, With Original Hooked Rugs, Designs and Patterns From Famous Museum Collections*. New York: Homecrafts, c. 1949.

Wiseman, Ann. *Hand Hooked Rugs and Rag Tapestries*. New York: Van Nostrand Reinhold Company, Inc., 1969.

Yoder, Patty. *The Alphabet of Sheep*. Raleigh, North Carolina: Ivy House Publishing Group, 2003.

Yoder, Patty, ed. *Green Mountain Rug Hooking Guild Dye Book*. Tinmouth, Vermont: Green Mountain Rug Hooking Guild, 2003.

Young, Arthur. *America Gets Hooked: History of a Folk Art*. Lewiston, Maine: Booksplus, 1994.

Zarbok, Barbara J. *The Complete Book of Rug Hooking*. Princeton, New Jersey: D. Van Nostrand Company, Inc., 1961.

Periodicals

Fiberarts, 67 Broadway, Asheville, North Carolina 28801

Rug Hooking Magazine, 1300 Market St., Suite 202, Lemoyne, Pennsylvania 17043-1420

Wool Street Journal, 312 Custer Ave., Colorado Springs, Colorado 80903

Membership Information

The Green Mountain Rug Hooking Guild began in 1981 when a group of dedicated rug hookers from Vermont decided to form a guild. Their purpose was to make it possible to meet twice a year, to share their joy of rug hooking, and to learn from each other and outside speakers.

As a new guild member, you will receive a packet of information which includes a full membership list, by-laws, a teacher and supplier list, and the most recent issue of our quarterly newsletter. We are able to provide you with a listing of members in your immediate area, and can refer you to representatives and teachers. Our newsletter keeps everyone current because many are unable to attend the fall and spring meetings. In addition to these benefits, members get to exhibit their rugs at our annual show. They can also participate in our education programs, getting materials and tools for their volunteer teaching efforts.

To join the guild, please visit our web site: www.greenmountainrughookingguild.org

Answer to the "Cabbage Rose Challenge" (found on page 138): Tony Latham.

Index

This index includes all rug hookers featured in both this book and its companion volume (noted here as "Vol. I"). Those with rugs in both books have the page number(s) identified for this book, plus the notation of "Vol. I" indicating rugs in the companion book as well.